TEENAGE GIRL POWER: PRACTICING JOURNALING AND MINDFULNESS

THE POWER OF A POSITIVE MINDSET TO BOOST
YOUR CONFIDENCE AND CHANGE YOUR LIFE

ADRIANA A. ROŞCA

© **Copyright 2021 Adriana A. Roşca - All rights reserved.**

The content contained within this book may not be reproduced, duplicated or transmitted without direct written permission from the author or the publisher.

Under no circumstances will any blame or legal responsibility be held against the publisher, or author, for any damages, reparation, or monetary loss due to the information contained within this book, either directly or indirectly.

Legal Notice:

This book is copyright protected. It is only for personal use. You cannot amend, distribute, sell, use, quote or paraphrase any part, or the content within this book, without the consent of the author or publisher.

Disclaimer Notice:

Please note the information contained within this document is for educational and entertainment purposes only. All effort has been executed to present accurate, up to date, reliable, complete information. No warranties of any kind are declared or implied. Readers acknowledge that the author is not engaged in the rendering of legal, financial, medical or professional advice. The content within this book has been derived from various sources. Please consult a licensed professional before attempting any techniques outlined in this book.

By reading this document, the reader agrees that under no circumstances is the author responsible for any losses, direct or indirect, that are incurred as a result of the use of the information contained within this document, including, but not limited to, errors, omissions, or inaccuracies.

Acknowledgment:

Book Cover Image Designed by Solomia Mendyuk (high school girl)

CONTENTS

Introduction	7
1. THE BEGINNING OF THE REST OF YOUR LIFE	13
It All Started with A Plan	13
The Feelings of A Teenage Girl	15
Overcome Overwhelm	20
Listen to The Voice in Your Head	24
Upgrade Your Skills	31
Courage from Birth	39
2. THE UPPER LIMIT PROBLEM AND YOU	43
The Upper Limit Problem	43
How to Get Rid of an Upper Limit Problem	46
3. UGH, DRAMA IS EVERYWHERE!!	51
Drama Is Intense	51
Drama Isn't That Dramatic	53
4. TEEN LOVE—A FAIRYTALE OR SOUL-SUCKING DRACULA?	57
Teen Romance	57
5. FORGIVE, FORGET AND LET GO	69
Forgive and Accept Forgiveness	69
6. YOUR LIFE MAP IS YOURS TO CONTROL	79
The Power of Me And The Method Behind Magic	79
The Right Decisions	81
Be Grateful	87
7. LET'S GET PRACTICAL!	109
The Art of Exercise	109
The Key is Proper Sleep	111
Volunteer in The Community	114

Find Your Opportunities 114
Quick and Effective Homework 117

Conclusion (Check the page after) 119
References 125

A girl should be two things: who and what she wants.
   −*Coco Chanel*

INTRODUCTION

The teenage years are probably some of the hardest years of your life, let's be real. A lot of the time, the glamorized versions you see on TV are nothing like real life. It's not all parties and adventure and finding your one true soulmate. It's stressful, it's emotional, it's difficult. You have schoolwork, homework, exams, friendship drama, crushes, emotions, identity problems, etc. It's meant to be a time of change and growth, but a lot of the time, we feel trapped, bored, and frustrated.

But that doesn't mean the teenage years don't have potential to be amazing. If you have the right mental toolkit, you can face any challenges that come your way! You can grow more confident and courageous and learn to love yourself. That's the purpose of this book—to give you that toolset. You'll learn about journaling, gratitude, forgiveness, and the skills needed to combat anything life throws at you! By the end of this book, you'll be able to see what I can—your future is mind-bogglingly bright!

Who says teenage girls can't be strong and courageous and do what they set their mind to? There are some amazing examples of teenage girls who do just that. In February 2013, when Megan Grassel was 17, she went out shopping with her younger sister looking for bras. She was shocked to find the lack of unsexualized, comfortable bras for young girls. "It dawned on me then that if no one else was going to make age-appropriate bras for girls, then I would find a way to do it myself". So, she set out to make them. She saved up all the money from her summer job as a waitress and raised over $40,000 on Kickstarter. She drew up designs and, shortly thereafter, she was able to start her bra company, Yellowberry. Yellowberry sold its first bra in January 2014, and by November 2018, had sold a million bras and has since been featured in Time magazine, Forbes, and on the Today Show.

The bras have little mantras sewn on the tags to honor Megan's late little sister Caroline, who died at just five years old. These mantras, she says, really capture the spirit of what it means to be a carefree young girl. Phrases such as "Go barefoot" and "Seek and find a hug when you need one" make up the backbone of the company.

Megan is clearly an example of a teenage girl who is empowered, resilient, and courageous. She stands by what she believes in and puts her skills to good work in the world!

Life is not all highs, though. There are some terrible lows. Sometimes, it feels like you are facing one difficult challenge after another. However, by being resilient, you can get through anything. You can learn from the tough times and come out the other side a stronger, smarter, braver person. You've got to keep going!

BE

FEARLESS

BE

YOU

In the movie *Gimme Shelter*, the protagonist, Agnes "Apple" Bailey, is a teenage girl with a very tough life. She runs away from home and realizes she's pregnant. The world deals her blow after blow, but in the end, she finds family in a shelter for teen moms. This movie is based on the true story of DiFiore, who quit her Wall Street job and opened up a shelter for pregnant teens, and director Robert Krauss' experience in living in said shelters for a year. It's a representation of life in a shelter and the resilience of the teenagers living within them.

There is unbelievable strength in being resilient, and there's also unbelievable strength in being yourself. You are you, and that's something no one can ever take away from you, no matter how hard they try. You are an entirely unique person with unique skills and passions. I know—it sounds so cliché, but think about it. No one exactly like you has ever existed in the history of the universe or in all of spacetime, nor will ever exist again. You're an entirely one-of-a-kind mix of chance, a self-formed by a million little things. Everything from the atoms that make you, to the way you've been influenced by who and what you love, is unreplicable. So, you owe it to both yourself and the world to love yourself and be as authentic as possible.

17-year-old Bliss from the movie *Whip It* is an example of a teenager who finds something she's passionate about that influences her understanding of herself. She is tired of her small, old town in Kentucky and her mom entering her in beauty pageants. When she sees a roller derby team in a local town, she is drawn in and decides to join them. She goes through many obstacles in order to play the sport she loves. In the end, she feels like she fits in more and has better relationships with those around her since she has finally found and followed her passion.

Believing in yourself and your passions is the most important thing you can do. Another cliché? Yes, but the truth in it is impossible to deny. Your potential is defined only by what you believe it's defined by. If you think you'll never succeed, you'll most likely never succeed. Why? Because you'll never try. But if you have a positive mindset, if you believe that your ability isn't a fixed thing, then you're more likely to succeed.

Say you and your best friend both fail a math test. Your immediate thoughts are, "I'm so bad at math. I'll never succeed. I might as well never try again," whereas your friends' are, "I didn't try my best at that test. I'm going to ask the teacher for more help and I'm going to go over my answers and see where I went wrong. I believe that I can do better!" Which one do you think will do better? I aim to share the secrets of this positive mindset with you because it's something that lies dormant inside each one of us, in need of unlocking.

The movie *The Freedom Writers*, which is based on a true story, provides a good example of this. The kids in the movie have all seen horrible things happen in life, and none of them even expect to graduate high school. They presume their lives will be one of gang violence and early death, so they don't even want to try. Their teacher manages to encourage them to write journals and, slowly, they realize that their lives don't have to perpetuate this violence. In real life, all 150 students graduated from school, became published authors, and many of them went on to graduate college and find success in great careers helping others!

What we can learn from this story is that the potential to be a better person, to be someone great, will always lie inside you. You just have to choose to see life from a different and new perspective. The future is not set in stone, it's something you can create all on your own. Your choices and decisions matter. This book will help you make the best ones you can.

I've been through a lot in my life. I moved from Transylvania, Romania to Chicago with my ex-husband. I managed to adapt quite well, and I got my Masters in Health Communication from Northwestern. I've been married, divorced, and in many long-term and short-term relationships. I've spent my life studying the field of self-improvement. I've been to many self-empowerment seminars, I've given talks to high school girls, I've had a life coach, and I've held women's relationship meet-ups. I'm so excited to share all I've learned with you! I hope my knowledge and passion blows your mind and makes your life outstanding, because helping girls achieve their goals matters deeply to me. I started writing this book because I realized the need for high school girls to raise their self-esteem and realize their power. It's important to me that you know that you are and always will be enough!

So, come on! Let's get into it! Let's start changing your life for the better, together!

1

THE BEGINNING OF THE REST OF YOUR LIFE

IT ALL STARTED WITH A PLAN

Everything seems chaotic when you're in high school. The drama, the homework, the crushes. Nothing fits in nicely; nothing slots together. It's just one big crumbly pile of uncertainty and more emotions than you feel your brain or body can handle. I've been there. There are little universals across the human experience, but the cringey, scary teenage years are one of them. You're lost and anxious, wondering, "What do I do now? What comes next, after I'm done with high school? Will things ever be the same again? Will they be different in a better or worse way?" There's no instruction booklet to handle everything that's going on in your life; there are no pre-written rules or precedents to the exact cocktail of experiences that is you. But there are similarities across experiences, no matter what walk of life you come from, and by sharing this research and my own experience of coming from a different culture, I have faith I can help you through.

> *Success leaves clues.*
>
> — TONY ROBBINS

There are steps to owning your life, to making all of this less uncertain. So, let's get to them! We'll start with planning.

When you're at this stage, you're probably not thinking of planning. I know, I know, you're rolling your eyes, groaning, and sighing at this already. "What do I need a plan for?" Sigh as much as you want, but let's be real, girl, you need a plan of action. Do you want to take the bull by its horns? You wanna show that you know what you're doing? Planning is what I wish I'd done in my high school years. Planning is what got me through my adult life. To dream is to want something badly, but dreams are nothing without plans.

> *If you talk about something, it's a dream, if you envision it, it's possible, but if you schedule it, it's real!*
>
> — TONY ROBBINS

That's my motto in life. It's all linked together, one big daisy chain of ideas-to-action. Don't wait to be pushed or for someone else to tell you how to do it because they will if you don't make a plan. And believe me, their plan will be a lot different than yours. But you'll still follow it because *you don't have a plan!* The importance of planning is something I wished someone told me in high school. But, hey, I'm here for you, so let's do it!! Dream and want and plan. Do it now, before you wake up an adult and realize you're not where you want to be. It's easier to form habits when you're younger than try and break them when you're older. Your actions today will likely become habits and influence you for the rest of your life.

The first thing to do when you're making a plan is to identify a goal. This can be anything, no matter how big or small! Maybe you want to become a doctor or a politician, or maybe you just want to spend more time with your grandparents. The most important thing is that it's something *you* want, not your parents or not your best friend. Write down the goal, then write a list of reasons why you want to achieve it—this will help motivate you! Next, write down the how. Brainstorm it! Just have general ideas at first, then once you've finished that, break it off into smaller step-by-step actions. Once you have a step-by-step plan, set a deadline. Then tape your written-up plan somewhere you'll see it every day and tell your friends and family so they can hold you accountable. Reward yourself when things go right, and analyze the situation, but don't be too harsh on yourself when things go in different directions. Readjust, focus, and change your approach until you get what you want.

THE FEELINGS OF A TEENAGE GIRL

How are you feeling right now? Angry? Anxious? Overwhelmed? Frustrated? A collection of emotions that you seem unable to define, all running together like the dyes off cheap fabric in the washing machine? No, it's not mind-reading, I've been there, and many other girls have too. I've been where you are; I've stood in your shoes in the midst of a hurricane of emotions. I too have gone through that time when my emotions seemed scary and confusing and overwhelming.

But, in the end, emotions are not scary, trust me. They're just chemicals in your brain, trying their best to react appropriately to the situations around you. In teenagers, the prefrontal cortex is developing, meaning you're probably experiencing new emotions, along with mood swings. This is all normal, including anxiety. Anxiety may seem the scariest of emotions, but it can be beaten. In the end, all your anxieties will just seem like little bumps in the road, I promise. They'll soon fade into the distance behind you. But sometimes anxiety can get the better of you and that's okay.

Have you ever watched the movie *Inside Out*? If you haven't, I'd definitely recommend it! I know, I know, it's a little childish. But it actually holds true to a lot of research done throughout branches of psychology. Many psychology students now study it as part of their course! In the movie, we get to see that every emotion has a purpose—fear is to keep us from danger, anger is so we know when we've been wronged, disgust stops us from being poisoned, sadness allows for empathy and compassion, and joy helps us to experience all the highs of life. All our emotions work together, and if we try to repress some of them, we end up repressing a lot more than we aimed to. The character of Riley in the movie is going through major changes in her life, and she tries to repress her sadness. This only leads to her repressing her joy as well and becoming irritable and depressed.

So, your emotions are important, but it's also important to be able to understand and learn how to manage them. In order to get a grasp on your emotions and how to get power over them, we first have to look at Plutchik's Wheel of Emotions. Yes, it's a real thing! It was invented by an American psychologist, Dr. Robert Plutchik, after studying emotions for years.

There are over 34,000 emotions that a human being can experience. That's right, 34,000! However, emotions are a lot like colors—there are a few primary emotions, and the rest are mixes of them or varying degrees of intensity. Most psychologists say there are anything from 5 to 27 basic emotions. Plutchik's Wheel of Emotion identifies 8 of them:

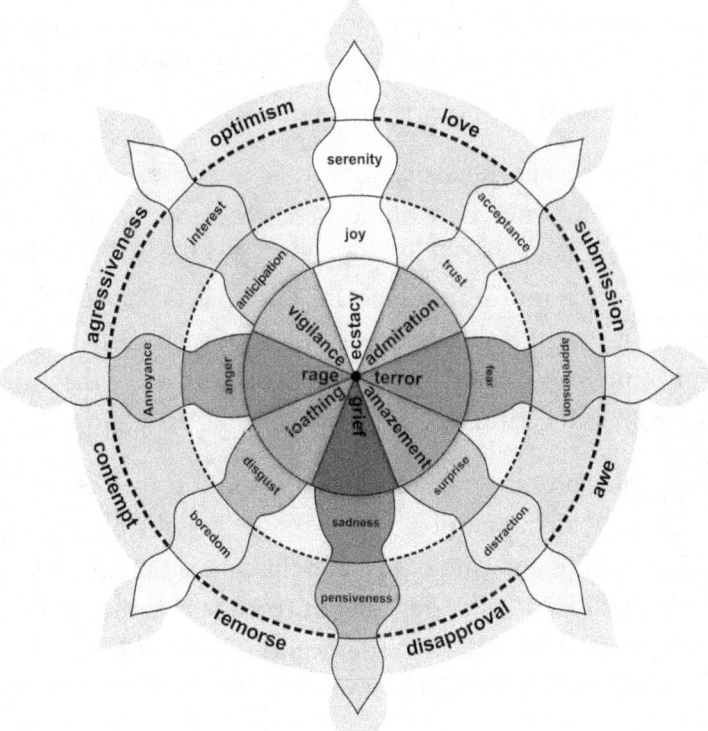

- Anger
- Joy
- Anticipation
- Sadness
- Trust
- Fear
- Surprise
- Disgust

In what situations would you be experiencing these emotions? Perhaps you may be angry at your parents for not letting you go out, or your teacher for giving you too much homework, or your friend for lying to you. Perhaps you may be joyful to make a new friend, or receive a present, or go to a concert. Perhaps you may be experiencing these emotions for what seems like no reason at all!

Then there's the intensity aspect of the wheel. There are varying ways you can experience each emotion, and if left unchecked, your emotions can grow stronger and stronger. Annoyance can turn into rage, for example, or apprehension can turn into terror. Therefore, it's important to be able to name and understand your emotions early before they turn into something more.

Each emotion also has an opposite emotion on the wheel. Look at which emotion is across from which emotion. Sadness is the opposite of joy, anticipation is the opposite of surprise, disgust is the opposite of trust, fear is the opposite of anger. All that makes sense, right? They're all equal and opposite reactions to situations.

Have you ever felt so unbelievably intensely, but been unable to put words to it? Maybe you're going through your first breakup or heartbreak and are having a hard time dealing with the anger, grief, sadness, and all the other emotions you're feeling. That's what Plutchik's Wheel of Emotion is for. The Wheel will help you better understand and come to terms with your emotions, which is what you need to do in order to cross this challenging water. To come to terms with your emotions means to gradually accept them. This will, over time, help you to move on.

Naming your feelings using the wheel is a great way to grow! It can help you achieve better self-acceptance and be more compassionate with yourself and others. Also, it can help you establish healthier relationships—if you can name what you're feeling, you can communicate it better to someone else and solve the problem together. They might be going through the same emotions as you, but either way, they'll be able to open up to you and name what they're feeling better! The great thing about the wheel is how it can simplify the concept of emotions, which is, oh boy, one difficult and complicated concept!

The best thing to do once you've identified these emotions is to write them down. Put them, and the story you tell yourself about them, in a journal, then come back a few days later and see if they are still there. Why are they still there, or why have they disappeared? Have they mutated into something else? Perhaps your emotions from a few days ago seem silly, or scary, or perhaps they seem just as real as they did back then. Either way, you can gather great knowledge of your emotions from writing them down. What triggers your emotions? What makes them better? Over time, you'll be able to understand them more and more, and, thus, they'll become less scary. Remember, *clarity and execution are power, not knowledge.*

OVERCOME OVERWHELM

It's really important to use the Emotion Wheel to identify how you're feeling—that's why it's here! Anxiety is a nasty little thing and it'll get in the way of truly finding what you want and getting it. It's on the emotion wheel near fear and the more you try to hide or push your emotions down, the worse it can become. In other words, it will mess up your plan! And that is one thing you don't want. What factors influence how anxious you are? There are many factors that can affect how anxious you are, such as past experiences, your current situation, your diet, and both physical and mental health challenges. Choosing empowering positive thoughts is an important one that you can control, as is rephrasing the questions you ask yourself. With Plutchik's Emotion Wheel, you can gain awareness of what's going on, and how to beat your negative feelings.

Steps to using Plutchik's Wheel to overcome feelings of being overwhelmed:

- Study the Wheel of Emotions
- Identify what you're feeling and what's making you overwhelmed.
- Find the pattern in your emotions. What do you feel more frequently? What triggers these emotions?
- How is your body reacting to your emotions? Do you feel tension anywhere? Are you tapping your feet or biting your nails?
- Awareness of what, why, and how you are doing something is one of the key factors in emotional intelligence and power. Learn to catch your

emotions in time, and how to express them healthily before they overwhelm you.
- In order to find patterns, write everything down and evaluate it later.

It's important to ask the right questions. Write down and answer these Empowering Questions in your journal. You can use them as a guide to who you are and what you want in life and come back to them whenever you feel overwhelmed or anxious.

- What can I do? (As an example, you could use your creativity to redecorate your room and create a beautiful, peaceful physical environment!)
- What can I control? The answer to this one is your thoughts, how you see the situation, and how you react to it.
- What is most important to me right now?
- What can I be grateful for?
- What other ways can I look at this situation?
- What value is there in these?
- What aspects of my life do I need to take more ownership of?

You may go through a lot of difficult situations in your teenage years and your life as a whole, be it break-ups, the death of a relative, failing an important exam, being diagnosed with an illness, moving homes, growing apart from a close friend, or your parents getting a divorce. There's nothing too big or small to have an effect on your heart. Your pain is always valid, and you are never alone. There might be times where you can barely think or all you can feel is pain and heartbreak. In any situation, it's important to know how to heal properly, so your emotions don't overwhelm you all the time. Here is some advice for faster, healthier healing:

- Don't rush how you feel about these kinds of real-life challenges. Don't set deadlines or try to limit the time you take to process your feelings.
- Try not to worry about what-ifs. Focus on the facts of the situation.
- Rely on loved ones for support. No girl is an island! Even if it's just them sitting with you in silence while you cry, or a string of paragraph-texts, it'll make it better. Your friends and family care more about you than you'd think.
- Hang out with friends and family and, after a while, stop talking about your challenges. Go out for a walk together, or to the cinema, or play video games together.
- Try to laugh it off when you make small mistakes instead of beating yourself up over it.
- Don't bottle it up. Go somewhere secluded and scream it into the wilderness if you can.
- Or you can write it down on a piece of paper. Burn it if you want.
- Start a new hobby that you've always wanted to do!
- Write down your negative thoughts and refocus on the positive, by finding the opposite word or feeling and writing it down beside it.
- Practice self-care. Make sure you're exercising, sleeping, and eating right, and perhaps do something relaxing, like take a bath or use a facemask.
- Practice gratitude. Focus on what you do have.
- Plan something fun to do to take you out of the disempowering, sad state of mind! Your state of

mind is your way of looking at things, and it can greatly influence how you feel about a situation. Here are some examples:
- A trip by yourself or with friends.
- A movie night or sleepover.
- Going to a gathering or dance
- Anything that makes you happy! Whether that's staying home and playing Minecraft, or going to town for a window-shopping spree, it's important that it gives you a positive, empowering feeling.
- Keep out of situations that make you upset, if you can, both IRL and online. Unfollow and block your ex if seeing their posts on your screen makes you want to throw your phone out the window. If parties make you uncomfortable, you don't have to say yes to every—or any—invite! Boundaries are your best friend. Remember, if you set a boundary with someone and they don't accept it, it's best to not have them in your life anyway. Boundaries are *extremely* important.
- Plan a future for yourself, look ahead to the life you want to live. It's okay if it's just a rough idea, or if it changes over time, but it's important to give yourself something to look forward to.

What's important to keep in mind, whatever the challenge is, is that healing is not linear. On Monday you could be top of the world and finally think you're over the problem, but by Tuesday you could be down in the dumpiest of dumps again. And that's okay. Really, it's completely normal to have an unstable recovery. But no matter how it feels right now, it *will* get better. Whoever said the teenage years were the best years of one's life must not have ever experienced them, because adulthood is full of opportunities for happiness when you start planning early!

LISTEN TO THE VOICE IN YOUR HEAD

No, I'm not crazy and neither are you. Having a voice in your head is an essential part of having a human mind. Sometimes the voice can be a productive, kind voice, a voice that can help you. But sometimes, it can do nothing but criticize you and bring you down. It's important to be able to distinguish between these helpful and harmful voices. Remember that *you* are the only one in charge of writing your own story. Not me, not your parents, or your grandparents or your friends. *You!*

The insecure voice is a voice you might hear in your head. Little Miss You-Will-Never-Be-Good-Enough is forever taunting you, comparing you against some impossible golden standard of a person. Self-critique can be good sometimes: it can push us towards a goal, it can give us good moral standards and it can help us become better people.

What's worse is when this self-critique happens too much, too harshly, or when it starts critiquing things that are way beyond your control. It can make us super-insecure; full of doubt and even self-loathing. You might be insecure about a whole manner of things: disability, weight, acne, skin color, voice, etc. Your eyes, your nose, your mouth, your body, your hair—the list is endless. Most of these things you can't control at all.

Wait a minute, why are we insecure about these things then? If we can't control them, why do we have insecurities about them? While the voice in our heads that judges us is just part of being human (and some people are more prone to it than others, due to both different life experiences and different brain chemistry), we weren't born with such specific insecurities. Instead, this physical image of the "perfect" person comes from the outside. Sometimes it may be because you were bullied for a certain feature, or someone made a comment about it once upon a time and you can't stop thinking about it. Sometimes it's more subtle than that.

Open up social media, turn on the TV, and you'll see it. This 'perfect' girl. Skinny with big boobs, lightly tanned, smooth hair, even teeth, sparkling eyes, clear skin, without any body hair so on and so forth. Over and over again, in half the shows you watch, on billboards, on your Instagram. In reality, there are so many things wrong with this 'perfect' image:

1. This woman is usually wearing make-up, has gone through plastic surgery, and is covered in so much editing and so many filters that she's unrecognizable. No one looks like that in real life.
2. Who even decides what's 'perfect' anyway? News flash: it's probably someone trying to sell you something. Some rich old man, head of a trend diet or makeup company, trying to create another insecurity so he can get money off you. The specific features that make this woman 'perfect' are not features that every human being is born believing are perfect. Social standards change rapidly over time, and they're quite often based on horrible ideas and leave entire groups of people out. Ew!!

In reality, your body is stunning. It's formed from the dust of dead stars that traveled across galaxy upon galaxy to reach here. It's made up of millions of intricate little cells, all working together to keep you alive. Your eyes, your nose, your mouth, your hands, and your feet, all super complex machines unlike any other. You are a miracle, an entirely unique product of so much unimaginable history. The freckles on your cheeks, that scar on your leg, even your acne and your awkwardness, it's all completely unique.

No one exactly like you has existed in the history of the universe nor will ever exist again. And what? You're gonna hate your miraculously working, fantastically intricate body because some millionaire on a billboard told you "this is the perfect body?" Because some kid in 4th grade made you feel not good enough? Beauty standards are not your friend. You should not aim to obtain them. Because it may sound harsh, but no matter how hard you work, you'll never be perfect by society's standards. And there's always someone in this universe who'll be better than you at something anyway. It's very much impossible and, no matter what, people will still not like you for things you can't control. By learning to love yourself and overcome your insecurities, you're not being stupid or idealistic, or self-obsessed. You're rebelling against all those who don't like you for reasons you can't control and you're giving the middle finger to that millionaire man trying to make a profit off you.

Honestly, how badass is that?

And you're not only giving your beautiful, hard-working, miraculous body its due respect, but you're being rebellious and awesome while you do it. You're also making it less likely that people will bully or pick on you. Let's face it, there are many reasons why bullies will pick on you, and self-esteem is one, both your low self-esteem and theirs. And, on top of that, if you learn to love yourself, you're less likely to be a bully yourself. You're more likely to be kinder to those around you, and confident people often attract more friends and even potential partners. You're more likely to be able to solve challenges better and deal with pressure.

Wow! That's a lot of upsides! But overcoming insecurities is a constant process. You don't just decide "I'm going to like myself today" and suddenly you do. Your insecure voice will never go away completely, yet, sure enough, it will learn when to shut up and take the backseat if you work on it enough. After a time, it'll fade into the background.

So, what are some things you can do to overcome that insecure voice?

- Take care of your own needs. Make sure you drink water, eat three meals a day, exercise regularly, take breaks from social media, get adequate sleep, etc. When your physical needs aren't met, it often drastically impacts your emotional state, whether you want to admit it or not.
- Affirm your own values. Think about all the times you've been smart, you've been kind, or you've helped people. There are probably a lot more than you'd think. And if you can't think of enough, it's never too late to start doing random acts of kindness! Helping others and doing things in line with your values can really help your self-esteem!
- Speak up for yourself. It's hard, of course, but it's worth it. Tell your own story; say what you need to say (at an appropriate time of course). You'll find it will give your confidence a huge boost.
- Limit self-criticism. Whenever that voice comes to

tell you you're not good enough, interrupt it. Tell it you don't care, because it's lying. Stop yourself every time you find yourself thinking negative thoughts like, "I hate myself," or "I am unlovable," and think more empowering thoughts instead. It may sound silly and more effort than it's worth but that's not true. All your thoughts and actions are controlled by neural pathways in your brain. The more you think certain thoughts, the easier it is to think them again, like flexing a muscle. So why not try thinking empowering thoughts and blocking disempowering thoughts? Even if you find it hard at first, and you don't have the emotion behind it, it will eventually cause your brain to start thinking empowering thoughts automatically and thus improve your outlook on life. And that's when courage and confidence build up!

- Feel all your feelings. Don't try to limit or bottle up your emotions. Let yourself be sad, be happy, be scared. It might feel uncomfortable, but it will definitely help you in the long term.
- Surround yourself with people who love you. Don't isolate yourself!
- Meet friends outside your normal circle, perhaps join a club! Meeting new friends is a great way to improve your social life, see how others look at life, and be open to hear or learn about life from different perspectives.
- Try going for a walk or listening to music. When you're stressed, these produce endorphins, or "happy chemicals," in your mind, which will help you calm down and make you more resourceful in finding solutions!

- Set small realistic goals to achieve daily. Simple things such as "feed the dog" or "write a diary entry." Everyone has things that are in or out of their limits, so make sure it's something small and achievable! You'll feel more confident and more productive when you're crossing stuff off your to-do list.
- Take action to move towards your bigger goal. Whatever it is, be it to become a nurse or to write a graphic novel, to travel the world or to connect more with your family, to make money doing make-up, or to embrace yourself without it, work on it! Don't pressure yourself, but take small steps towards it every day, be it saving up money or researching how to achieve it best. Find a way; get resourceful.
- Write out your negative thoughts. Then come back to them and view them objectively. Why are they wrong? If you still think they are right, what can you do to change the circumstances, to become better? Write an opposite word beside the negative one. How does it feel?
- Accept compliments. Because, girl, those boots really do look great on you! You really are smart and funny and kind. Don't try to brush it off!
- Accept what you can and can't control.

There's also the failure voice, that inner-saboteur who will tell you that you'll never succeed no matter what you do. Don't worry, everyone struggles with hearing this voice at one stage or another. I know I sure did. Become aware of this voice and aware of the thoughts that are limiting your growth. It's important to focus on the present moment and truly live in it. Stop worrying about the future. It's not set in stone in the same way the past is. Those future self-sabotage thoughts you have are not real; that didn't happen, because you are in the present, not the future. The past doesn't equal the future unless you live there.

> *When you are not honoring the present moment by allowing it to be, you are creating drama*
>
> — ECKHART TOLLE

Another example of a voice that might inhabit your mind is the self-aware one. Yes, girl! This voice is able to see all the parts of your mind and how they work together—or don't. While too much self-awareness can make you awkward and anxious, in general, this is a good voice to listen to. It's best to acknowledge all parts of yourself, good and bad. If you never notice what you're doing wrong, you'll never find a way to fix it! This voice can see behind the nasty self-destructive thoughts that the other voices produce. You can develop your self-aware voice by taking a step back from your thoughts and analyzing them from a more rational perspective.

> *Don't believe everything you think. Thoughts are just that —thoughts.*
>
> — ALLAN LOKOS

Have you ever seen *Gossip Girl*? It's about a mysterious blogger uncovering truths and spreading rumors about the rich and popular girls at her school. Of course, I'm not telling you to start gossiping. Absolutely do not do that! But this mysterious blogger was making these rich kids aware of their self-destructive behavior. They appeared kind and genuine in front of the camera, but in reality, they weren't. *Gossip Girl* is a story about awareness of the self. It's important to develop your self-awareness, in order to get a full understanding of your own identity and habits you have that you mightn't be aware of.

There are many different frameworks you can use to get to know your true self. In this book, I'll cover a few of them, but there are many more out there, much more to fit in one book. Self-discovery is a constant process because the self is a constantly changing thing. While self-discovery is an important part of being a teenager, the need to know yourself doesn't stop when you grow up. If we don't grow, we die. Life is unpredictable, always changing, and we have to learn and adapt. Change is automatic. Progress is not. Progress is the result of conscious thought, decision, and action.

UPGRADE YOUR SKILLS

How to give good advice:

- Don't judge the other person. We all make mistakes. Even if you don't agree with what the person has done, try to have empathy with them and put yourself in their shoes. It's brave that they even came to you to open up! Try not to let your own opinions and biases affect the situation.
- Be honest. Don't pretend to be an expert on the situation.

- Wait until you hear all the facts before you give advice. It's important to know the full picture! If someone asks you questions halfway through, deflect them until the story is finished being told.
- Ask questions. Ask them why they took certain actions, why they feel the way they do, what *their* opinions are on the question. If you ask the right questions, they might get to see things in a new light or come to a conclusion. This is called the Socratic method of thinking and it's a great way to challenge ideas and come to conclusions about the problem.
- Ask if they want advice before intervening! We all know that one person who gives unwanted advice at every opportunity. They mean well, of course, but it's soooo annoying. Sometimes people just want to express their feelings without needing any advice.
- Don't just say the first thing that comes to your head. It's important to think through and consider all your options. It takes time to think things through.
- Walk them through the options. Repeat the options they gave you back to them (to make sure that both you and they understand what they're telling you!) and evaluate those options after that.
- Help them see things from the outside. Sometimes we get so caught up in our little details that we can't see the bigger picture.
- Give any information you know about the topic, be it from research or personal experience. Remember, don't pretend to be an expert! If you know resources that may help them, point them in that direction.
- Try not to hurt their feelings! Sometimes people do need tough love, but it's important to be as gentle, polite, and considerate as possible with them, even if

you believe they are in the wrong. If you hurt their feelings, they may consider this a betrayal and not take your advice at all.
- Do NOT suggest anything that would harm your friend or other people.
- **If you're genuinely worried your friend is in harm's way or might hurt themselves or others, seek professional help. Tell an adult you trust or call a hotline. Do not try to keep those challenges to yourself.**
- Catch in with them at a later date to see how the problem is going.

How to Deal with Challenges

Some of the challenges we deal with in life have simple solutions. And that's great! But a lot of them don't. To deal with these challenges, we need problem-solving skills. It can be hard to work through a problem, but the more you work on it, the easier it becomes. So how do we do it? An easy acronym you can use to remember how to solve a problem is IDEAL:

- **I**dentify the problem
- **D**efine your solutions
- **E**xplore your options
- **A**ct on the best option
- **L**ook back and reflect

Identifying the problem is the first step. Your problem may seem too big and complex to tackle at first. Write it down, break it into parts until it seems manageable.

Next, focus on what solutions you want- maybe your problem is you want to buy concert tickets, but you can't afford them. In that case, the solution might be to think of ways to get more money! Also think about the context of the problem, where it fits into your life. It may be bigger or smaller than it first seems!

In order to explore your options, it's important to brainstorm. Be as creative as you can; write down everything that you think of. Even if the first answer that pops into your head to get more money is "find a pot of gold", don't limit yourself! Once you're sure that you've finished doing that, start evaluating, and cross off the silly ones or anything that won't work. Examine the consequences of each of the options you have left— write a pros and cons list!

After you've done all that, it's time to pick the best one! It might take a while, or it might be obvious. Either way, it's ok! There might not even be just one of the options—it might be a combination of two or more of them. Make a decision and put the plan into action. It may be hard, but you've got this, girl!

After you've finished your action, it's time to look back and evaluate. Did it go as you thought? Keep doing it that way then! If it didn't work well, what would you change if you were to do it again? And then, try another solution. Remember that problem-solving, like all skills, is something that takes a lot of time to practice, so don't be discouraged if it doesn't work well straight away!

Write Everything Down

Keep a list of everything you've accomplished in your life, big or small. This'll help you understand where your skills lie and how to improve them and build on them! Use as much detail as possible. For example, you may be good at spelling, make-up, cooking, math, reading, researching, listening, designing or you may still be friends with your 2nd grade bestie! Impressive! Whatever your unique abilities are, when you put them into work, you'll fly (metaphorically)! Look into your skills on a deeper level. How can you apply them in your own circles? Find what details make up that skill—peel it like an onion! You can ask your friends and family what they think you're good at too.

Go back to your childhood. Think about all the stressful situations that you survived. Write down the statement "I'm at my best when..." and fill in the blank. Write in all the details—every single accomplishment, no matter how small. This is the list of your successes, be sure to keep failure out of it! We all have strengths and weaknesses, and it's important to be able to identify your strengths and build upon them.

Everyone is a genius. But if you judge a fish by its ability to climb a tree, it will live its whole life believing that it is stupid.

— A QUOTE LONG ATTRIBUTED TO ALBERT EINSTEIN

Use the SWOT analysis! Draw a table. In one corner, put Strengths; in one, Weaknesses; in one, Opportunities; in the last, Threats.

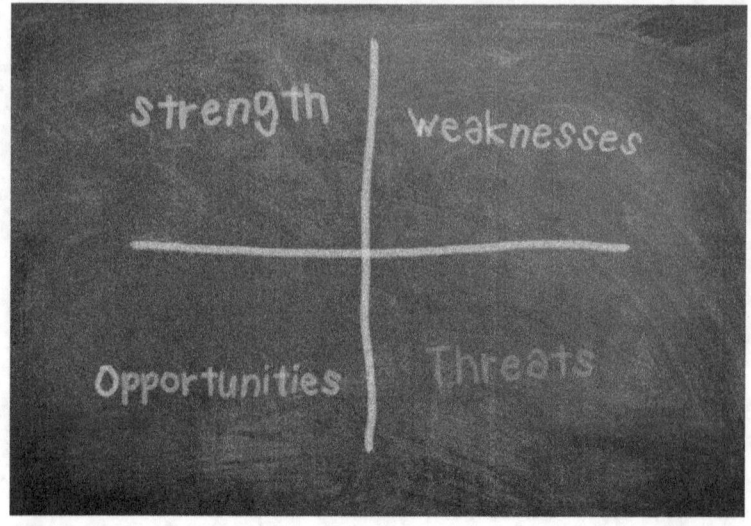

If you're having challenges with identifying all of those, here are some example questions you can ask yourself:

Strengths:

- What achievements are you most proud of?
- What do other people see as your strengths?
- What are your core values and how do you show them?
- What strengths would you like people to praise you for?
- What do you learn easily?
- What do you like about yourself?
- What are some unusual skills you have?
- What do you like doing and why?
- How have you overcome obstacles in your life?
- What gives you energy?
- What in the world would not be the same if you weren't here?

- There are also plenty of tests online that can help identify your strengths and weaknesses!

Weaknesses:

- What do people say you need to work on?
- What have been your major challenges and difficulties in life?
- What things do you usually avoid doing due to a lack of confidence?
- Do certain personality traits tend to hold you back or cause challenges?
- What bad habits do you have?

Opportunities:

- What do you want to accomplish this year?
- What are you grateful for in your life?
- What small step could you take right now to make a change in your life?
- What is one thing you could do to improve your well-being?
- What challenges can you find solutions for?
- How can you develop your skills?
- Who are the important people in your life? How can they help you?
- What resources do you have?
- How can you turn your strengths into opportunities?

Threats

- How are things changing around you?
- What are your major challenges right now?

- In what way can your weaknesses affect your progress?
- Do any of your strengths hold you back?
- Could one area of your life affect the others?

Tap into Your Past

Can you remember one of the best things that ever happened to you? Out of every moment in the history of you, what was one of the happiest? What day could you never forget? Try to get that memory to the forefront of your head, as vivid as you can get it. Then grab a pen and paper and start writing it! What was it? Did you win a medal for fastest runner in gym class? Did you have a birthday party, and all your friends were there? Did you perform in your school play? Did you finally give that bully a piece of your mind? It doesn't matter what it is, how silly or trivial it may seem from the outside. This is about *you*.

Paint that picture in your mind very clearly. It will help you a lot, to be able to go back to those feelings whenever you're feeling down. There are three important things to focus on and write down in order to get you into the state you were in that moment:

Your posture: How did your body look during this scenario? Did you jump up and down or run around the place, full of energy? Swing your arms or clap your hands? Were you standing strong and confident and proud? Did you hug someone? Really try your hardest to visualize this. It's important to develop this skill of self-awareness.

The mood: How did you feel? Was it an energetic, exciting sort of happiness, or a more serene euphoria? Were you proud of yourself? Were you thankful? Use Plutchik's Wheel of Emotions to help you! How did your emotions influence how you reacted to the scenario?

What you said: Can you remember saying anything to someone else about how great it was? Was it "OMG!! I did it! I'm unstoppable!" "Thank you so much!!" or "We won!!!" Did you just let out a squeal or a giggle of happiness?

COURAGE FROM BIRTH

Courage is a fantastic thing to have, especially for a teenage girl. In order to achieve anything, we need the courage to do it. We were all born with a little gold nugget of bravery deep in our allegorical heart, but sometimes it gets buried with fear along the way. But don't worry, it's still there! Everyone still has that nugget, deep down. You can get the confidence to do whatever you want to do, big or small! Let's get tapping into that courage!

There is only one way to become courageous: act courageously. Even if you don't feel courageous, acting with courage will produce miracles! You'll feel better, stronger, more confident. Courage is the one thing where you can truly "fake it 'til you make it!" You'll gain more confidence and higher self-esteem. You become more competent at what you do. Being courageous is like a muscle doing a certain exercise—the more you act courageously, the easier it is!

> *If you choose courage, you will absolutely know failure, disappointment, setbacks, and even heartbreak. That's why we call it courage. That's why it's so rare.*
>
> — BRENE BROWN

In order to be courageous, you need the courage to take the action, the commitment to planning it, the capability to get more info, and the confidence to believe it with all your heart! Here is some advice for each of these steps.

Courage to take the action

Courage is inside you already, just remember that. It's not something anyone else can give to you or take away from you.

Don't be afraid to be afraid.

> *Courage is not the absence of fear, it is the ability to act in the presence of fear.*
>
> — BRUCE LEE

Courage is not about being big and tough and scary. It's about being true enough to yourself and compassionate enough towards others to stand up for what's right. What takes the most courage is being kind. Practice being kind as much as you can.

Commitment to planning it

Be committed enough to plan an action.

Examine the situation. Sometimes you'll realize that that's all it takes to prompt you into action because doing nothing has a much more negative effect than doing something!

Don't be afraid of failure. It's just another learning opportunity.

Study your capabilities and resources

Look into the situation. See what you can do, and focus on that, not what you can't do.

What talents and resources do you have that could help in this situation?

Don't be afraid to ask for help! Who do you know that could give good advice on this?

Confidence: believe it with all your heart

> *Believe in yourself! You may have a fresh start any moment you choose, for this thing that we call "failure" is not the falling down, but the staying down.*
>
> — MARY PICKFORD

Let go of what you can't control and focus on what you can.

Congratulate yourself after being courageous. If you're happy about it, you're more likely to do it again.

Practice, practice, practice! Courage is a skill you have to learn, like riding a bike or playing the piano. And you learn it by being courageous!

2

THE UPPER LIMIT PROBLEM AND YOU

THE UPPER LIMIT PROBLEM

Do I Have The Upper Limit Problem?

You've probably never heard of the Upper Limit Problem. If you have—well done, girl! If you haven't, it's quite an easy concept to grasp, don't worry. You'll probably find that you've experienced the Upper Limit Problem before!

Let's look back at your past experiences:

Have you ever worried about what other people think of you? If not, you're certainly in the minority. Are you sure you've never thought that people were judging your outfit walking down the street, that people were whispering behind your back on the playground or that your friends secretly don't like you?

When you get emotional (look back to Plutchik's Wheel; it could be any specific emotion or a whole bunch of them!), do you tend to blame or criticize others? You may even be doing it without thinking.

Does your insecure inner voice talk to you a lot? Does it tell you that you simply aren't good enough? Does it make you question your choices, your style, anything, and everything about you?

If you've answered yes to any of these questions, then you may have the Upper Limit Problem. Don't panic, but you could be subconsciously sabotaging your own happiness!

Why Do We Do It?

Hold up, hold up, I know what you're thinking. "Me? Sabotage my own happiness? Never!" Honestly, it happens more than you'd think! Most people struggle with The Upper Limit Problem at one point in their lives or another, or even for longer. Not everyone is aware of it! Why, though?

Well, according to Gay Hendricks, Ph.D., people often have limited tolerance for happiness. Everyone has an inner thermostat, usually programmed in early childhood, that determines how much love, creativity, and success we allow ourselves. This is controlled by four root subconscious beliefs: "I am fundamentally flawed and don't deserve success," "If I succeed I will end up all alone," "I am a burden and success will make me even more of one," and "It is wrong to be better than others." Do you ever find yourself having thoughts or feelings along these lines? Oftentimes we don't even notice!

When we get too close to what we want, these beliefs trigger something within us, perhaps fear, anger, or even physical illness, in order to stop us from succeeding!

Some Examples

Your math teacher tells you, "You'll never pass math!" and you start to believe passing math is impossible. Instead of putting in the effort to pass, you don't study because "what's the point?" and, thus, repeatedly fail math. Even when you try to study, your mind just won't let you!

You spent weeks preparing for your part in the school play or talent show, but the night before, you get ill and can't perform! If this happens once or twice, it's probably just bad luck, but if it happens almost every time an important event comes up or you have to make an important decision? It's probably an Upper Limit Problem.

Pause your reading for a few minutes. Think of a time or times where any of the above situations or similar ones happened in your daily life. It might be an Upper Limit Problem!

Signs you might have Upper Limit Problem

- **You Are Constantly Worrying:** If you worry about everything, particularly when good things are happening in your life, then it might be because of an Upper Limit Problem. If there's something you can control about what you're worried about, then take positive action, but if there's not, try your best not to worry about it.
- **You Often Blame and Criticize Others:** When you blame and criticize others, you are causing drama

and limiting your own growth. Try to take what positive action you can or communicate calmly, instead of blaming other people.
- **You Are Drowning In Guilt:** You may feel guilt over things you did, didn't do but thought of doing, or even about being happy. Remember that it's pointless to think about these things now. A good way to stop guilt is by stopping accepting automatic thoughts, and by questioning "Why?" every time you feel guilty every time you did or didn't do something. Keep asking yourself why, in order to really get to the root of the problem. (There's more about guilt in Chapter 5)
- **You Keep Listening to Your Negative Thoughts:** Saying "I don't know if I'll be good at this" is your brain's way of dealing with potential failure. You're judging yourself for potential successes or failures before anyone else gets the chance to. Have the courage to push through your negative thoughts!
- **You Push Your Successes Away:** Have you ever felt like every time you do something good, you start pushing it away? Perhaps you get into a good friendship, only to start an argument or isolate yourself. Perhaps your application for a summer job finally gets accepted, but on the first day, you decide you're too good (or not good enough) for this place.

HOW TO GET RID OF AN UPPER LIMIT PROBLEM

The Ultimate Success Mantra

One way to try to get rid of your Upper Limit Problems is meditation. I know what you're thinking: "That sounds so hippy-dippy and boring!" But meditation has been validated through so many scientific studies that its effects are hard to deny! Not only can meditation help you with your Upper Limit Problem, but it can also help in relieving multiple physical and mental health conditions, as well as in relieving pain! It can improve attention, memory, and your ability to take in new information. Long-term meditation can help you bounce back from stress easier. It can make you more compassionate, improve your relationships, reduce your biases towards other people. It's not a cure-all for every problem in life, nor does it work for every single person in the world, but considering it's got all these benefits, and it's safe and healthy to do, you can't say it's not worth a shot!

Different kinds of meditation work for different people and different challenges. One way to meditate is with a mantra, which is a phrase, often in Hindu, that's repeated over and over again. This can help us connect with ourselves and the life we really want. It can help us become happier and more fulfilled! Gay Hendricks gives us an "Ultimate Success Mantra" in his book "The Big Leap," which is meant to help with Upper Limit Problem.

I expand in abundance, creativity, success, and love every day as I inspire those around me to do the same.

— GAY HENDRICKS

So, how do we meditate with this Ultimate Success Mantra?

You can do this meditation every morning or every evening. It'll only take about 5 or 10 minutes a day. Remember that it may not work at first, and that's okay. Meditation often takes time. Try to find a comfortable space in your house, with as little noise and distractions as possible. Noises outside the window, like cars on the road outside, or a neighbor mowing their lawn, shouldn't matter. Learning to accept these noises without them dominating your thoughts is an important part of meditation, but your little sibling talking to you or your father watching TV in the same room will probably affect you. Sit on the floor on a cushion or blanket or on a chair, whatever is most comfortable. If you want to sit outside, you can, but make sure it's in a quiet enough place! Try to wear comfortable clothes as well. Put your phone aside, and turn it on airplane mode, it's just for a few minutes! Decide on how long you want to meditate for.

Once everything is set up and comfortable, close your eyes and become aware of your breath. Breathe into your nose and out of your mouth and out a few times, until you feel relaxed and "in the zone." Start repeating the Ultimate Success Mantra over and over again. Really feel the mantra, imagine your love and creativity expanding inside you and inspiring your family and friends. Repeat the mantra for a few minutes, then focus on breathing for another ten seconds. Just let any thoughts come, even if they are "this is silly" or "what a waste of time." Remember these thoughts are proof it's working! Just listen to them without judgment. If you're doing it for ten minutes, after about five minutes, you can take a break and focus on breathing for about 10 seconds, before returning to your mantras.

Stay Open-Minded and Question Everything

There are a few other things you can do on top of that to keep an open mind and battle your Upper Limit Problem.

First, focus on this message: *I'm committed to discover and learn more about my ULP and be open to having fun with it! It is an attitude of wonder and cheerful thoughts.* Repeat it to yourself, be it out loud or in your head.

Remember deep down, that you are allowed to be happy. You are allowed to be successful. You are allowed to take up room, to show the world all the talents you can offer it!

Everyone has their Zone of Genius, no matter how ordinary you feel. Your Zone of Genius is the things you do that make you feel at home. It's the skills that play a key part in your identity. You can use your great talents to change not only your own life but the world! Here are some questions to determine where your genius lies:

- What work do I do that doesn't feel like work?
- What do I love to do for long periods of time?
- In my day-to-day life, what do I do that produces the most satisfaction in the least amount of time?
- What am I good at in unusual times? What abilities of mine come to light in new, stressful, or uncertain situations?

Remember those Empowering Questions from earlier? (page 21) You can always go back to them. They can help you with your Upper Limit Problem too!

Live Long and Prosper.

— STAR TREK

3

UGH, DRAMA IS EVERYWHERE!!

DRAMA IS INTENSE

Drama, Drama, Drama

Drama is everywhere in high school! But why on earth do people create drama? For every drama queen, there's a different reason. It may be because they are trying to run away from the real challenges in their life, it may be because they grew up in a household full of drama, it may be for attention or it may simply be because they like the excitement or the joy of having a story to tell. A lot of people who spread drama don't know who they are and what they want in life. If we look at the broader picture, that's the story of a lot of people in high school. No wonder drama is everywhere!

Drama can be a very wild ride. It can be hard to keep on top of who isn't talking to whom, who has a crush, and who's fighting with their parents. With homework, study, and all the other pressures of high school on top of that, everything becomes very stressful very quickly. That's normal though! Most people go through a lot of drama in their teenage years —if you don't, count yourself one of the lucky few!

Even the most trivial of things will cause drama. It all accumulates, and you really can't avoid it. It just happens. Don't panic! In what ways can we deal with this?

How to Diminish Drama

- Assess the situation. What is it in your life that is bringing you a lot of drama? Your love life or the love life of your friend? Arguments with your parents? Fights in your friend group?
- Remember to breathe! Take deep breaths, in and out. This will help keep you calm.
- Break your challenges down into separate little steps. Don't try to tackle the monstrous pile of challenges all at once! Let's say you're facing slipping grades, an argument with a friend, and problems with a teacher. It will make you tear your hair out trying to solve all these problems at once. So, prioritize! Which one's most important right now? For example, let's say you want to start with the grades. What can you do? Study more? Get a tutor? Ask a friend or a teacher to help you? Only after you solved that should you move on to the next problem,
- Something I would often do to minimize drama is to zone out and try to imagine the place this problem will occupy in my life in a week's, a month's, or a year's time. Put your thoughts as far away as you can, and you'll often see how small this problem is in your life and in the universe.

- Be honest with yourself, is it you that's repeatedly creating drama? Why do you think you're doing that? Is it for attention, excitement or to keep yourself from having to deal with some bigger issues? (If you find it's you, there's more advice later in this chapter)
- If you did something wrong, acknowledge your mistakes and apologize. Do it in person if you can, rather than over text. It's easier to show you're sincere when they can see your face!
- But don't blame yourself for everything! There are some situations that are honestly out of your control. Remember you're not responsible for the actions of others and criticizing yourself for them will only end up with you being either further away from your own inner peace.

DRAMA ISN'T THAT DRAMATIC

Don't Feed The Drama

Remember, just because someone creates drama around you, doesn't mean you have to feed it or participate in it! Often people say things just to get a reaction. Next time someone invites you into their drama, be it by trying to start a fight with you or by complaining to you about someone, take a moment to stop and think. Ask yourself, "Do I want to be emotionally involved in this drama?" "Do I have the energy?" and "Does this benefit anyone?" If the answer is no, try to be calm and reasonable about the matter, even if you're angry. Respond politely, and don't let them get any emotional reaction out of you!

> Build a reputation for not participating in drama
>
> — ADDY RODRIGUEZ

Avoid the Label 'Drama'

Sometimes, you need to tell the difference between drama and an actual problem. Things like bullying, bigotry, and harassment or trauma, for example, should never be dismissed as just drama. Oftentimes people are overdramatic, sure, but if someone seems genuinely distressed instead of just gossipy, it's important to be kind and to be a good listener. Even if the reason seems small to you, remember that everyone has a different brain and different experiences, so there's no reason to mark it as 'petty' without even listening to the story, especially if the person is upset. What we dismiss as drama could be someone who genuinely needs our help.

Start labeling things as 'challenges' instead of 'drama.' This will help you solve the problem, instead of simply "spilling the tea" and gossiping about it. There are some challenges that can be solved very easily, but drama often drags on and on and on for no real purpose other than people want to perpetuate it.

> Don't speculate, good or bad. Simply deal with what's actually in front of you.
>
> — MICHAEL STODOLA

Be a friend to the person and don't judge them or their challenges. Don't judge people if you want to influence them in a positive way. Judging people can close the door to acceptance and love. Instead, just listen. (For more advice on being a good listener, see page 31). Then, be a friend to yourself and don't worry about the problem or let it take over your life. A lot of the drama in life comes not from the actual experiences, but from what we think about them after the fact.

How to Stop Creating Drama

So, you've looked at the situations involving drama in your life and you realize that there's been one common factor—you. Don't panic! Try to catch yourself when you're spreading gossip. Do you find yourself repeating the one name over and over again, for example? Change the subject if you find you've been gossiping for too long. Ask yourself if complaining about them is really making the world a better place. Is it really their fault? Is what this person has done something that you have also done in the past? Look for a solution to the challenge, instead of complaining about it. If this person is toxic, can you cut them out of your life? Can you reduce the time you spend with them? Can you come to an agreement between the both of you? When you are telling stories, make sure they're real. If you exaggerate, things can quickly escalate out of your control. And don't continue talking for ages, either.

Use Drama as a Life Lesson

Drama is an inevitable thing in life—sometimes we just can't escape from it. It happens to everyone. To avoid all drama is to avoid human connection, to isolate yourself completely, to never hold any opinions. And, trust me, I don't recommend detaching yourself from life completely just to avoid drama.

So, what can we do but learn from it?

What things can we learn from drama? We can learn how to move on and not hold grudges. We can learn the importance of self-acceptance and not caring what others think about us. We can learn about communication and healthy relationships. We can learn how to better deal with drama the more we deal with it. Whether it's your friend's crush dating someone else, or two people having salty insult-battles, analyze the situation and see what you can learn from it. It's often a lot!

4

TEEN LOVE—A FAIRYTALE OR SOUL-SUCKING DRACULA?

TEEN ROMANCE

Teenage love can be difficult and complicated. Even knowing whether or not you have a crush on someone can be surprisingly, staggeringly hard. The crushes themselves can take over your life and last for what seems like an eternity. And relationships? They can break many hearts, even if you're careful. This can result in low self-esteem and trust issues. Uuuugh, believe me, those trust issues can last well into adulthood!

Not everyone has romantic relationships in their teenage years, so don't worry if you don't find your first partner until adulthood or in the end, romance turns out to be not for you at all! There is no default way to do it. For those who do end up in relationships as teenagers, it's scary. This is no fairytale or cartoon, where you have one big kiss that saves the day, and suddenly you're living in happily-ever-after-land. You're probably gonna make mistake after mistake. You simply don't have enough information and experience with relationships yet. That's ok. Now's the time to make mistakes. You can learn so much from them!

I'm not saying that you shouldn't take part in relationships at all as a teen! Far from it, you just gotta be careful. There are ways to do it that reduce the chance of your heart being blown into a million pieces. When it comes to teenage romance, it's different for everyone. Some don't want it at all. Some would rather wait, or they just can't seem to find that special someone. To some, romance is their whole world, and to some, it's just something new to try! There are a few challenges that a lot of people who do engage in romance have in common, though.

Are You Ready to Date?

Perhaps all your friends are in relationships, perhaps you're the first of them to date. Either way, you've found what seems like the perfect person for you. But are you really ready for a relationship? Or are you just feeling pressured to get with someone? If you enter a relationship without being emotionally mature enough, it can cause a lot of damage to both you and the other person. Different people become ready at different paces, so don't worry if you find that you aren't ready yet! Here are some questions to ask yourself to see whether or not you're ready.

- Do you really want a relationship or do you simply want one because everyone else has one?
- Do you know your boundaries? Do you feel comfortable with hand-holding, kissing with tongue, or taking your clothes off? You *don't* have to feel comfortable with any of these things to enter a relationship, but you need to *know* what you're comfortable with. You can't make these things up as you go. You need to be strong enough to say "no, I'm not comfortable with that" when the time arises.
- Do you think you could handle a break-up well? Do you think you could deal with the pain of being broken up with or the awkwardness of breaking up with someone else?
- Do you really like this person? Why? If it's just because they're attractive or because they showed interest in you, then it's probably not strong enough to last. Do you genuinely want to spend more time with them?
- Do you have the time and energy to spend on this relationship?
- If you've been in a relationship before, are you over your ex?
- Do you feel comfortable talking about important and difficult topics with them? If no, then you simply

won't be able to have a relationship with them, as relationships require a *lot* of communication on difficult topics.
- Do you have interests and ambitions outside of finding romance? It's important you both have your own interests outside the relationship. It can lead to a very unhealthy relationship otherwise. And never *ever* give up your goals for someone else.
- Are they right for you? Try not to date anyone more than a grade older than you. Even small age gaps in the teenage years can lead to massive gaps in experience and maturity. Girls are more likely to be pressured into things they aren't ready for if they date someone significantly older than them.
- Will your parents let you date? If not and you really like the person, how can you convince them? Don't start an argument, instead, show how mature you are.
- Are you looking for someone to complete you? If so then you're not ready. You're a human being, complex and complete already. You do not need to be fixed, or even to fix someone else. And if you do need help with your self-esteem, you are not going to find it in a relationship. You want someone to be by your side, someone you can be yourself with. Two whole beings, not two parts of a whole.
- Do you have a healthy relationship with yourself already? Do you like yourself? Do you do things that make you happy? If you don't have a healthy relationship with yourself, it's very hard to be in a healthy relationship with someone else.
- Do you realize that it's not gonna be all rainbows and flowers? The honeymoon phase will wear out, and

there'll be good and bad days. Are you ready to deal with that? There's no point idealizing the relationship.

How to get over heartbreak

- Allow yourself to truly feel your emotions. Don't try to bottle them up or shove them down. Don't try to rush them or limit them. Just let yourself feel.
- Cry!! Cry!!! Don't be afraid to cry!!
- Make a playlist of your favorite break-up songs!
- Keep a diary.
- Talk to your friends and/or family about it and be open to see and learn from any advice.
- Seek the positive in the situation. Remind yourself that you're better off without this person, though it's good to have loved at all. Ask yourself what you've learned from this relationship. Are there parts that you would like to still experience or avoid in future relationships?
- Think about the downsides of the person. Were they mean? Were they self-obsessed? Did they talk too much? It sounds unfair, but it has been scientifically proven to help, when combined with the other strategies listed here.
- I know it sounds harsh, but sometimes the best option is to cut this person out of your life. Block the person on social media. Don't send them texts or try to call them. Try starting up hobbies that don't involve them. Set your boundaries for better healing.
- After a while of thinking about it, try thinking of other positive thoughts. Think of how lucky you are, how blue the sky is today etc., There's always

something to be happy about if you look hard enough!
- Try meditation.
- I've said it again and again: make self-care a priority. Make sure you're eating, sleeping, and exercising right.
- Treat yourself! Buy your favorite food, or that book or top you really wanted, or watch your favorite movie! Take a bath or do a face mask. The possibilities are endless, whatever makes you happy.
- Try to see the situation from a neutral perspective, if you can, or even from the other person's shoes.
- If you're sad over a breakup with a boy, it may seem like he's moving on quicker. In reality, men often hide their feelings more than women do, due to social pressures, so he's probably still hurting deep down. And in the end, he did you a favor. Would you really like to be in a relationship with someone who's uncertain about you? Who won't make you a priority?
- It will probably take a couple of months. Let it take its time.
- Plan something to look forward to!
- Learn to forgive. (For more information on forgiveness, see Chapter 5)

Avoiding Unhealthy Relationships

The most important thing in a relationship is that it's healthy, and for that, good communication is necessary. Most arguments and challenges can be solved by clear communication. The communication needs to be ongoing, as well as mutual. Clearly communicate your wants, needs, and boundaries. If they overstep your clearly stated boundaries that's a clear red flag that they don't respect you and you should probably run for the hills!

Some other red flags that should make you wary are:

- They try to limit who you hang out with without a clear reason. And, no, unless you are clearly flirting with someone else, jealousy is not a reason! They say, "I don't want you to talk to other boys" or "you should leave your friends." You should try to make sure you have a support group outside the relationship—a social circle of just you and they means you don't have anyone to talk to if things go downhill. Plus, we are all social creatures, and it's healthy when both partners have time apart to spend alone or with their own friends!
- One or both of you hold grudges and repeatedly bring up past mistakes, instead of sorting them out as soon as possible.
- Being passive-aggressive instead of just saying what's wrong. Making someone guess how they hurt you, instead of, you know, just telling you what's wrong and working through the challenge together. Not only is that behavior frustrating, but it's also toxic and can cause someone a lot of stress. Because you can't find a solution if you don't even know what the problem is.
- They influence you negatively and pressure you in ways that they shouldn't. Have your grades dropped since you met them? Have they been mean to other people, and expected you to be mean too? Have they tried to pressure you into drinking alcohol, smoking,

or vaping, or even taking other drugs? That's a definite warning sign of a toxic relationship.
- They don't respect your emotions. If you tell them that you're scared of something, they laugh at you and continue doing it. If you start crying, they don't comfort you, and instead, call you a crybaby.
- They mock you, and it goes far beyond joking. They make you feel insecure or even worthless. They even do it in front of other people!
- They say that you'll never find someone else or that you're lucky to have them
- They are dismissive of your interests, or even your goals in life.
- There is a significant age and maturity difference between the both of you that causes difficulties.
- You don't feel comfortable around them.
- They guilt you often.
- You feel trapped in the relationship.
- They never admit it when they're wrong.
- They cheat on you.
- They pressure you into doing things in the relationship that you don't want to, e.g. having sex.
- They raise their hands like they're about to hit you in arguments, or, even worse, they have physically hurt you before.
- They lie repeatedly or steal from you.

While one of these things, once, (depending on the context) might just lead to a serious talk about their behavior, if they do these things repeatedly, then run, girl, run! If you find you're the one doing these things, then it's time to take a look at your behavior, figure out why you're doing these things, and try to change them. This list doesn't just apply to romantic relationships—sometimes friends and family members can be just as guilty!

Even if the relationship is not outright toxic like the examples on the list, it can still be unhealthy. So, how do we make our relationships as healthy as possible?

If I have an issue with someone I go straight to them to talk about it, and I don't talk to anyone else about it if they aren't involved. Gossip breeds drama!

— KRISTIE SHERMAN

The old saying is true—we do become who we surround ourselves with. "Our self comes to include the people we become close to," as psychology professor James Coan put it. Our brains tend to mimic that of those we are close with, numerous studies have shown. Oftentimes, we may find ourselves feeling other people's emotions without realizing it! In fact, even if it's just through social media you interact with, other people's emotions can still affect you.

So, it makes a lot of sense that you need to choose who you interact with carefully. If your core values aren't aligned, it will cause a lot of problems within the relationship. Remember, you only have enough emotional energy for enough drama in your life. Ask yourself which relationships make you happy, and which drain you of more energy than they're worth. Which of your friends are people who you admire, and which would you never want to be? If you don't feel comfortable cutting people out of your life completely, try minimizing the amount of time you two spend together. If you're having a hard time deciding who you should keep in your life, try writing in your journal about how you feel about people and analyzing it.

Keep people close to you that give good advice and help you see things from another perspective. Stick around people who encourage your goals, and who may have similar goals themselves. It's important to receive constructive feedback on things like schoolwork or art, so, for that reason, try to find people who are as passionate about whatever you like as you are! Not that all your friend groups should be a monolith of people with the exact same interests, opinions, goals, and ideas though. It's important for your growth as a person to be able to see other perspectives as well as debate new ideas in a safe environment.

Try to avoid people who encourage you to make bad decisions. Go with what you feel is right! Avoid people who try to change you into someone you know you're not.

Sometimes it's hard to cut people off. I know because I found that hard too. It's especially hard if the people you're trying to distance yourself from are your family, because, well, most teenagers literally live with them. If you can't cut yourself off from people who cause drama and hurt, then recognize what triggers it and try to avoid that thing, be it mentioning another person or a certain topic. Try not to bring it up in conversation and respond as calmly and objectively as you can when it does come up.

Keep those around you who say what you *need* to hear, and not just what you want to hear. A lot of drama comes from confusion and poor communication. Eliminate it by having the courage and honesty to say what you really mean, and the strength to be open to genuine criticism. If someone feels like they need to walk on eggshells around you, they'll likely hold a lot in, and this will lead to problems in the relationship down the line. On the flip side, tell people what they *need* to hear. Obviously, don't be rude about it, but constructive criticism is the way to go! If something that they've done upset you, don't hold it in. As I said before, don't assume they know what they did wrong; no one's a mind-reader. And *don't* bottle it up so much you become passive-aggressive. As the old saying goes, "the truth will set you free."

Journaling About Love

Why don't you try writing in your journal about love? Here are some questions you can ask yourself:

Have you ever been in love before? Perhaps you're currently in love! If not, when was the last time you felt it? What does it mean to you to be in love? How does it feel? What do you look for in a partner? Is it important that they are fun and have a sense of humor (which is the most important personality trait to a lot of people)? Or do you value intelligence or style or perhaps physical attractiveness? Is there a pattern to the people you fall in love with? Do you tend to fall in love with mysterious strangers, for example, or close friends? Perhaps you've never been in love. What do you imagine, then, that it would feel like?

5

FORGIVE, FORGET AND LET GO

FORGIVE AND ACCEPT FORGIVENESS

All About It

Who hasn't been hurt by someone before? It sucks, but it's something that happens to most people. You may feel insulted, betrayed, or lost. It may be from an acquaintance or even an 'archnemesis,' but it could also be from a loved one. Be it a friend, a partner, or family, sometimes those we hold dearest are the ones that cause the most upset in our lives when they don't treat us with the proper respect and kindness. Forgiveness is about letting go of the hurt of the past. It's not about forgetting or glossing over the seriousness of what happened, oh no, and it doesn't mean returning to the same relationship with that person at all. Instead, forgiveness is something you do for yourself. It's about making a conscious decision to let go of your resentment surrounding a situation.

Why should you bother forgiving someone who hurt you, though? Well, forgiveness can help you embrace hope, gratitude, and joy. Forgiveness has been scientifically proven to reduce depression, anxiety, and hostility, as well as giving you higher self-esteem and greater life satisfaction. It can improve our physical health too! People who are more forgiving are more protected from the negative effects of stress, such as high blood pressure, as well as having stronger immune systems. It can give us healthier relationships, improve grades, and make us more empathetic. Letting go of the past can help you focus on the future, giving you room to grow. Plus, who wants to spend all their time thinking about someone who hurt you, and probably doesn't even think about you back? Do you really want them to occupy your mind? Are you really going to give them your power? Unforgiveness hurts you and no one else.

Resentment is like taking poison and waiting for the other person to die.

— MALACHY MCCOURT

The Act of Forgiveness

Forgiveness is the ultimate act of self-care, and it's something we can extend to ourselves as well as others. It's hard to be happy when you're bogged down with feelings of rage and resentment, or guilt and self-loathing. Forgiveness can alleviate these feelings, and help you release that life is something that happens *for* you, not *to* you. You can stop being haunted by the past and move on to your brilliant future.

Although it's definitely worth it, forgiveness is not a linear path, and it won't be the same for every person or for every situation. There's not some magical one-size-fits-all spell you can do and suddenly forgiveness is all around you. But don't worry, the hard work will be very much worth it.

It's important to determine who harmed you and how you've been harmed. It may seem obvious what it is, but sometimes you do need to dig a little deeper to get to the root cause behind it all. Remember that you don't have to forgive someone if they didn't hurt you, for example, if you just thought they were annoying. However, it is often good to start by forgiving small things first, in order to build up your empathy. If someone accidentally breaks your pen or says something rude to you in passing, you can recognize the wrong straight away and then recognize that they probably weren't directing their negative attitude or carelessness towards you on purpose. From there, you can forgive them. "This way you also can learn to immediately stop the negative reaction and the feelings that come with it," says Dr. Tyler Vanderweele of the Harvard School of Public Health.

Is there someone in your life you haven't forgiven yet? The first thing you can do is write it all out. First, write how you really feel or felt about the situation, and then write how you can find it within yourself to forgive them. Write a letter of forgiveness; it's therapeutic, even if they never read it. It will hopefully help you to move on and forgive the person.

Empathize with the person who's hurt you. Try to imagine why they hurt you and what they might be feeling. A lot of research has indicated that seeing the situation from the other side can make you more likely to forgive, and less likely to act out at the other person. I'm not saying that you need to justify what they've done and put their emotions above your own, just that you should try to understand what state of mind they might have been in when they hurt you. Seek peace, not revenge. The person who hurt you may never get their just desserts, but this is about *you*, not them.

Barriers to Forgiveness

What barriers may stand in the way? Well, you simply might not be ready to forgive, and that's ok. You're not obligated to forgive someone right away if they really hurt you. Things will get better with time. It may not heal all wounds on its own, but it will certainly dim the pain eventually. And then you'll be ready to forgive and heal some more. Some tips to get over this unreadiness are imagining the moment you want to forgive and yourself in it as vividly as you can, and to feel all the physical sensations that that action brings you. Does it give you a churning in your stomach or burning in your chest? Become aware of all this, and of your thoughts surrounding the situation, about both the other person and you. Ask yourself some questions about the situation then. What could you have done better? What could the other person have done better? What can you do from now on? Learn from this. Then, when you feel you're ready, you can forgive—however long it takes you.

You could be afraid of being hurt again. This is a legitimate concern. Remember that you have *every* right to set boundaries in your relationships. Whether you want to spend less time with the person or you want to establish "ground rules" to prevent this from happening again, it's important to set boundaries that make you comfortable. Remember that if someone rejects or oversteps your boundaries, they're not worth your time anyway.

You could be embarrassed to forgive them. You might be worried about being a 'pushover.' A good way to overcome this barrier is to boost your self-esteem. You need to develop a good sense of self, one that is completely separate from and unaffected by the bad things people say about you. This will take time, but you will find it not only easier to forgive, but you'll also see improvements in every area of your life. And it's an upward spiral—forgiving people can boost your self-esteem as well. An exercise to gain a strong sense of self that you can do is as follows:

- Sit comfortably (See the instructions on Upper Limit meditation for more advice on how to get comfortable for meditation). Focus on your breathing.
- Once you are calm, think about someone you feel safe around. It could be a parent, sibling, relative, teacher, friend, therapist, a spiritual figure, or even your own wiser self. Imagine yourself facing them. See the love and acceptance in their eyes and the kindness in their body language. Allow yourself to feel this warmth.
- Now imagine you are the other person, looking back at yourself. Feel the love that person has for you. See the goodness that they see in you. Let it radiate through you, this knowledge of your own goodness.
- Then go back to yourself, with the person still across from you. Notice where you feel their acceptance in your body. Are you smiling? Is there a warmth in your chest?
- Take a moment to think about it. You are reaching towards a positive version of yourself. Remember to

save these emotions and access them whenever you need them.

As you learn to forgive, you are no longer a victim of the events of your life. Trust me: life happens *for* you, not *to* you. People don't remember what you told them, but they remember how you made them feel when you talked to them.

The REACH Method

As well as having an easy-to-remember acronym for a name, the REACH method of forgiveness has been supported by many scientific studies and used by everyone from high schools to international peacemaking efforts! It also can help reduce symptoms of anxiety and depression.

Recall: Recall the event from a neutral perspective. Don't view the person negatively or paint yourself as an angel victim. Feel all the feelings that come along with this scene; don't try to push anything down.

Empathize: Empathizing with the other person, as explained earlier, is an important part of the forgiveness process. Ask yourself why they hurt you without minimizing the pain. Perhaps you may find that it's not personal, they were just having a bad day.

Altruistic gift: Think of a time you did something wrong and were forgiven. That's right, no one's an angel! How did it feel to be forgiven? Realize that forgiveness is a gift that we can give to others.

Commit: Write a letter you don't send or a journal entry or tell a friend. Commit to forgiving this person.

Hold: Hold onto your forgiveness. This is a hard part because the memories will come back. Remind yourself that forgiveness is not about forgetting and erasing these memories, but about changing your reaction to them. If you need reminders, you can revisit the letter or journal entry.

Self-Forgiveness

So, we've covered what to do when someone harms you, but what about when you harm someone else? We all make mistakes. Perhaps you made a comment you didn't think through until it was out of your mouth, or perhaps you were angry and shoved someone. Maybe you feel like it's haunting you, whatever you did. The inability to forgive yourself may lead to self-destructive behavior. But, at the same time, just forgiving every bad thing we do right away can reduce our empathy. So how are we ever meant to forgive ourselves?

Some psychologists differentiate between guilt and shame. Guilt is a feeling that you've done something wrong, and it's a healthy feeling that's important to feel. Shame is when you feel like you are a fundamentally bad person, that you can and should never be forgiven. Shame is unhealthy and can often lead to a myriad of problems. Self-forgiveness means recognizing and letting yourself feel your guilt without succumbing to shame. Like forgiving someone else, self-forgiveness is not about minimizing the situation or pretending it didn't happen, nor is it about pretending you are in the right. It's about learning to feel better about it over time. It's about moving on emotionally and not being caught in this one incident forever.

First things first, it's important to feel your guilt. Guilt serves a purpose—to facilitate change. Acknowledge the bad you did, and don't deny it. Don't try to pass the blame to someone else. Accept responsibility. Write it down or say it aloud if you need to! However, recognize that doing a bad thing doesn't make you a bad person. If you think you're a bad person, studies show, you're more likely to do bad things. You did a bad thing, and that's that.

Note: Sometimes, if you are dealing with trauma, loss, or mental illness, for example, you might feel immense amounts of guilt or shame over things that were either extremely small mistakes that hurt no one, or things that weren't your fault at all. These things do not warrant feeling guilty, nor do they need self-forgiveness. Try listening to your reason and fighting the guilty thoughts with more logical ones when they pop up.

Understanding why you did this thing can be important in moving on. Was it simply a careless mistake? Did you hurt someone because someone hurt you? Did you act out because you were afraid? Try to get down to the root cause of it. Use our old friend Plutchik's Wheel of Emotions to help you! This will not only lead you away from shame and towards self-compassion, but it will help stop you from doing whatever it is you did again, as you can deal with your feelings in healthier ways.

Once you've felt and dealt with your emotions, apologizing and/or making amends is the next step. This isn't always possible. The person may not want to talk to you. In that case, tell them that you're there if they want to talk sometime in the future, but you respect their decision. If you can though, always apologize. Apologies can remove the guilt and shame. They can also help you learn from your mistakes, and they will help you communicate with the person better if that's what they want. Not apologizing when you are wrong can be damaging to relationships. If they do forgive you, that's great! However, don't expect them to forgive you right away, or even at all. You are never entitled to anyone's forgiveness and you certainly aren't entitled to have the relationship back the way it was. The boundaries they set are their decision.

Apologies aren't just the word 'sorry' or, even worse, "I'm sorry that you feel bad." You have to be sincere, or there's no point doing it. A good apology has the three R's: regret, responsibility, and remedy. Express your genuine regret. Show empathy toward the person and how it impacted them. Say something like "I really wish I could take it back." Take responsibility. Admit to them what you've done wrong. Don't accept the blame for parts that weren't your fault but do *not* push the blame on them. For example, "I'm sorry for being mean to you but you were mean first" is not a proper apology. Apologizing just to get an apology in return is selfish and manipulative. They can apologize in their own time; this isn't a race or a show of who's the better person.

Try to think of ways you can make it up to them then and offer to do them. If you broke something of your sibling's, for example, you could offer to buy them a new one or to fix it. If you forgot about your friend's birthday, perhaps you can buy them a present or hang out with them for the day. It could also be a promise to change your habits, so this action won't be repeated again. Perhaps you might need to think before you speak more; perhaps you need to take a moment to calm down with deep breaths when you're angry. An apology might also be a good time for you both to discuss boundaries in the relationship going forward.

A face-to-face conversation is best because they can hear the sincerity in your voice, but if you feel you absolutely cannot do that, a long, well-thought-through message will do. Or even write them a letter and give it to them! As long as the apology is sincere and you include the 3 Rs, it's certainly better than nothing.

After apologizing, continue focusing on growth. Remember that absolutely everyone makes mistakes. You can't change the past, but you can change the future. You can do that by focusing on becoming a better person. Be kinder to yourself.

If you are religious, an important step in self-forgiveness is to ask your God for forgiveness. If you're not religious, but you're a generally spiritual person, perhaps try asking about nature, humanity, the universe, etc. You could either do this at the start or the end of the forgiving process, whichever feels right for you.

6

YOUR LIFE MAP IS YOURS TO CONTROL

THE POWER OF ME AND THE METHOD BEHIND MAGIC

The Decisions

The decisions we make today, though we often don't notice, have a million different consequences which reflect in our tomorrow. It sounds ridiculous, but it really isn't. Have you ever seen a time travel movie or tv show? If you have, then you'd know that every single action one makes in the past can affect the future in massive, unseen ways. Right? That's the rule of time travel, you can't talk to anyone, you can't knock a single thing out of place, or who knows what would happen. You knock over a glass of water, and suddenly when you go back to the present a monster is taking over your town! Such a small decision actually sent you to a different timeline, a different part of the multiverse. Well, it makes no sense to not apply that butterfly effect to the present as well! The actions you make today have an undeniable influence over the future, big or small.

> *I do believe that one way to have a destiny is to choose one.*
>
> — MELINDA MCGRAW

Our reactions to what life has in store for us are very significant. We can't just sit around and wait for stuff to happen. We can't wait for destiny to take the wheel. Even doing nothing is a decision that can affect our lives in many ways. Taking a "neutral option" because you're scared is still a choice, and it's still a choice that will affect the future. We must take control of our lives. Of course, not everything is in our control, but you often have control over more than you might think at first.

Sometimes you might expect more of life than you put into it. If you want anything, you have to make decisions. If you expect something without desiring it enough to put in the energy, then you're bound to be disappointed, unfortunately. If you just float around, letting life lead the way, you're likely not to get what you want out of it. Just hoping for something is not a proper strategy at all. You must grab every chance! You must research what you want!

> *It is not in the stars to hold our destiny, but in ourselves.*
>
> — WILLIAM SHAKESPEARE

THE RIGHT DECISIONS

There are three major patterns impacting our emotions, and these emotions in turn impact our decisions. This is our physical stance, what we focus on, and the language we use.

Your Physiology

Your physiology is the easiest of these things to control. Researchers at Harvard have found that power-posing can influence your performance at important events such as presentations and interviews. That's right, even just changing your body language before the event can have a massive influence on how you perform!

But what is a power-pose? A power-pose is a stance in which your chest is up, your shoulders are back, and you are open. In other words, you're taking up space! It makes you not only appear more confident, but feel more confident, and that in turn influences how you perform. Strike the pose for two minutes before an event you need more confidence in, such as a performance, a test, or talking to someone about something important. You'll find it may help your performance a great deal!

Some questions to write in your journal:

- Are you going to give up or keep going?
- What action (or lack of action) are you going to take in response?
- Are you going to change your posture? Are you going to stretch when you become upset? Stretching can improve your mood. Whatever bad mood you're in, don't stagger in it!

What We Focus On

You are in charge of deciding what you deem right or wrong. You are in charge of how you react to situations. You are the *master* of what you say and do and don't you ever forget it! It's you who chooses to either help or hinder your growth and your Upper Limit Problem especially. Don't project it onto other people. Don't lose control and blame others. Even if someone is mean to you, you should always try to be the better person instead of reacting negatively and continuing the cycle. You need to be able to control what and how you think about it.

Focus equals feelings.

— TONY ROBBINS

Here are some questions about focus that you can put in your journal. Remember that what you focus on in a situation greatly impacts how you feel about it.

- Are you focusing on the past, present, or future?
- Are you focusing on yourself or on the opinions of others?
- Are you focusing on anger and resentment, or are you learning to let go?
- How important is this thing you're focusing on to you?
- Do you see this experience as a failure or a chance to grow?

Where focus goes, energy flows.

— TONY ROBBINS

The Language Used and The Meaning You Give to Your Thoughts

We give meaning to everything that we do or think. How we understand and deal with our thoughts can have an impact on your decision-making abilities. When you get a thought, think "is this thought empowering, or is it a downer?" If it's empowering, great! Keep the thought! If it's a depressing thought, then put it in your brain's (metaphorical) trash can. Throw it away! If you want to change your life, pay attention to the words you repeat to yourself. Is it phrases like, "I can't do this," or "I'll never be anyone important!" that pop into your head? Or is it phrases like "I got this!" or "I know I can do this!" If it's phrases like the first two, try to interrupt the thoughts with some more empowering thoughts. Like I said before, neuro-pathways are formed every time you think of a new thought, and every time you think about it, it becomes stronger. The brain is like any other part of your body—the more you train it, the stronger it gets.

Believe it or not, our language defines our reality. The language and words you speak influence how you experience the world. To what degree, scientists and philosophers are still debating, but it's definitely true to say that your language —the words you use daily—influences your reality as well as your reality influencing your language. A lot of languages, for example, label colors differently. If you had been born into a language that had no concept of "orange" and instead had expanded the definitions of "yellow" and "red," would you know what orange was, beyond a yellowish-red or a reddish-yellow? Probably not. And it wouldn't be a big deal to you, either.

And that's just a small example. The same principle applies to everything. If you had no word for love and therefore no preconceived notion of what love was, no media displaying it, no expectations, would you love the same? Would it be like the English language, one little word, one big feeling, the same for your friends and your family and your dog and yourself and your crush and nature and the universe? Or would it be 2 or 3 or 4 or 5 or 20 different feelings? Or would every single time you feel it be different, an infinite number of words to describe an infinite concept? Would you love at all or would you just call it joy and compassion?

Another example would be the separation in the English language between people and nature. There's such a huge distinction between the way we talk about humanity versus the way we talk about our 'environment'. The phrase literally comes from the French word for 'surround'. As a result, people are often seen in English-speaking countries as being separate from nature, and this can sometimes cause people to have more lax attitudes to the world around us, even going as far as justifying environmental damage. However, in a lot of indigenous languages, for example, the Maori language, this distinction isn't as clear or made as often. Instead, humans are caretakers of the land and are deeply connected to it. It becomes harder to justify ecological damage when you see yourself as simply another part of the ecosystem—because then you'd be destroying yourself.

> *The words you attach to your experience will become your experience.*
>
> — TONY ROBBINS

So, now knowing just how much language defines our reality, what are some questions we can ask ourselves about language in our journal?

- Does this word or phrase serve me well or not?
- Which words am I using daily that aren't creating an empowering space for me?
- How can I use more empowering words daily?
- Can I change the intensity of the negative words I use? E.g. saying "don't like" instead of "hate," saying "a bit sad" instead of "depressed." Do you see the difference in the intensities of these words?
- Change the questions you ask yourself habitually, and you will change your life. For example, you may catch yourself asking the question "Will I get derailed?" Is this an empowering question? How about, instead of that, you ask yourself "How can I make this happen the way I want it?" It's so much better, right? It gives you space to find a solution.

The Takeaway

Tony Robbins says, "If you don't control these three decisions, you simply aren't in control of your life." It is vital that you sit down with your journal and a pen and write down what you are focusing on, what meaning you give to these focuses and what actions you are doing to make a change in your life. Write what you choose to focus on from now on if you're changing what it is you want.

These factors are what contribute to both your emotional state and your physical state. The emotional state and the physical state are intrinsically linked. If you change your physical state, your emotional state often changes with it. This makes a lot of sense, considering your brain is what controls your body! And both of these states impact our decision-making processes.

Like Tony Robbins is fond of saying, the questions that you ask yourself can greatly impact how you view the world. You *must* ask the right questions! An example of three questions he gives is:

1. What is something I can do for someone else today?
2. What is something I can do to add value to the world today?
3. What is something that I can offer to other people?

Ask yourself these questions every morning, and eventually, you'll see a shift in how you view your life! Some more questions are:

- What is something that I can do for myself today in an empowering way?
- What am I excited about?
- What am I grateful for?
- What makes me proud?

BE GRATEFUL

Are you truly appreciating the present moment? Do you think you can? If not, why not? What has to be changed? It's important to find gratitude.

Well, what is that? Gratitude is, according to Robert Emmons, a leading researcher on the topic, comprised of two parts:

"First, it's an affirmation of goodness. We affirm that there are good things in the world, gifts, and benefits we've received..." The second part is when "we recognize the sources of this goodness as being outside of ourselves."

Gratitude is when we realize that there is good both in the world and in our personal world, and that good comes from family members, friends, strangers, even a higher power. In other words, it doesn't come from us. It's nothing we can feel proud of, just thankful for. But it is very important to be thankful for these things. The benefits of gratitude have been noticed for centuries, and are a major part of most world religions, as well as being backed by the latest research in psychology and neuroscience. But what are the benefits? It turns out there are plenty. Here are some of the benefits of gratitude:

- Gratitude brings us happiness.
- It makes us feel more connected to the people around us.
- It can help in alleviating anxiety and depression.
- It helps our physical health as well, strengthening our immune system and reducing blood pressure as well as encouraging us to exercise more.

- It helps you sleep better.
- It makes you more resilient.
- It makes us kinder and more compassionate, often leading you to pay your luck forward.
- It is motivating and energizing.
- It strengthens our relationships.
- It makes us more forgiving.
- It makes us more likely to engage in self-improvement behaviors.
- It makes us humbler.
- It can help you notice and work on your flaws.

Let's face it, we are powerless over what happens in life. We are powerless over the thoughts of other people and their actions. We are powerless over all the shitty things that happen in the world every day. Disasters happen all the time. People get sick and people die. There's not some magic spell you can say to be free from pain. I wish with all my heart that there was, and I could give it to you. I wish there was a way to make ourselves immune to every bad thing. I wish there was a way to stop every horrible event around the world before it happens. Unfortunately for everyone, there simply isn't. You can't control these things. Life is unpredictable, no matter how well we plan.

However, you can control how you react to these things, and the stories we tell ourselves about them. Life is meant to be lived. It's meant to be lived authentically, completely, freely, full of feeling and love. The great philosopher Heraclitus once said that you cannot step into the same river twice. That is to mean, life is constantly changing. It is never the same as it was before, and it will never be the same again. In what other ways is life like a river? Well, it's true that we can't just walk against it. We can't redo the past, we can't stop events from happening. We can just adapt and go with the flow. You must focus on the now in order to have a great future.

The Words of Change

Everyone is trying to change for the better. Some look towards personal growth, some want to love themselves, and some people look for external validation. There comes a time where you need to stop second-guessing yourself and focus on the five words of change popularized by Tony Robbins. "I love you. Thank you."

This is adapted from the ancient Hawaiian process of 'Ho'oponopono' (pronounced Ho O Pono Pono), which is a ritual that dispels the poison of all that isn't love and the true self from one's life. It has been used for thousands of years to solve problems and to keep in touch with one's own authentic identity. Tony Robbins' words are a shortened version of Dr. Ihaleakala Hew Len's adaptation, which goes "I am sorry, please forgive me, thank you, I love you." Though the words must be exact, they can go in any order.

Saying these words might not change the person you are saying these words to. But they will change your perception of this person. These words are some of the most meaningful in the English language. They are so simple; they are phrases we use in our everyday life. Yet they can bring about great change. Try saying them to your parents or your friends or even to yourself in the mirror. Soon you will radiate compassion for both yourself and the world around you!

It's important to love yourself, though it's equally important not to put down anyone else to do it. That's not proper self-love. In fact, being kinder to yourself often makes you kinder to the people around you! Remember, you are a part of the world, not apart from it. To love oneself is to love the world, to love the world is to love oneself.

But just conforming to the expectations of others, just being exactly what everyone else wants from you, is far from love. You are not the idealized version of you that exists in some people's minds. You are complex, a unique collage of every experience that has shaped you and of those that came before, an amalgamation of all that you love and have loved and will love. Being your true self is something you owe not just to yourself but to the world. You're not a 1-Dimensional cardboard cutout of a person; you're not the 'popular' girl or the 'perfect' A-student or any other expectation someone throws at you. You are not anything you don't want to be. You are an individual that has never existed before and never existed again, and you belong as a unique self in the patchwork of things. You have skills and passions, you have thoughts and opinions, you are entirely your own person and you should let yourself shine as bright as you can. The entire world will benefit from it, I promise.

If someone does not want me it is not the end of the world.
But if I do not want me, the world is nothing but endings.

— NAYYIRAH WAHEED

Pain is inevitable but suffering is not

— TONY ROBBINS

Pain happens to everyone in life. But suffering is what happens when we think about that pain through the wrong lens. Our beliefs determine our perception of the world around us. If we believe that suffering is inevitable, that the world is inherently bad and that no-one likes us, then we begin to see this as truth, as our reality, and thus we suffer more. But if we believe that whatever bad state we're in, we can focus on improvement and we can get out of it. If we believe that pain is temporary, this becomes the truth as well. This breaking down of our thoughts, beliefs, and feelings about a situation in order to feel more positively about it is actually the basis for Cognitive Behavioural Therapy (CBT), the most popularly used and scientifically validated type of psychotherapy. It's so important to break and replace our negative thoughts and beliefs.

The stories you tell to reinforce your negative beliefs often begin at a loss, e.g. a breakup, or a less, e.g. not getting a grade you wanted. This leads to a 'never.' Say, for example, you went through a break-up and were feeling sad about it. You start to often think to yourself, either consciously or subconsciously, "I mess up all my romantic endeavors. I will *never* be able to find love. Why do I even try?" This dramatically decreases your self-esteem, you stop going out with friends, you become withdrawn and extremely self-conscious. The story you tell yourself is one of both self-hatred and self-pity, of you as an unlovable monster. But this isn't the truth.

You can change the suffering in this situation by changing the story you tell yourself. Instead, tell yourself that relationships end all the time, this doesn't reflect on you as a person and that all you can do is learn from this. Write it in your journal. Interrupt your negative thoughts with these realistic ones. You'll start feeling more optimistic about the future. You'll start hanging out with your friends again, perhaps start joining clubs or focusing more on school. And because you do these things, your life will improve. Makes sense, right?

Our feelings control how we experience the world, and we have the power to choose what meaning we put on these feelings. We have the power, then, to change how we experience the world. We have the power to take action to try to change our feelings, when that seems wise. We have the power to defy others' expectations, and we should, because expectations often lead to nowhere but disappointment, unfortunately.

Being selfless has been shown as having huge links with happiness. It's important to be able to see yourself as part of the world, an entity that reacts and relates with other people. Having tunnel vision focuses on yourself and your thoughts can only do so much, and it often leads to both you becoming selfish and you sinking deeper into negative thoughts.

Suffering comes in your perception of the fact, not the fact itself.

— HARRISON BARNES

Of course, it's a bit harder than this—simply because the thoughts won't go away immediately. You will have to keep reminding yourself again and again. It will be hard, but trust me, it's *so* worth it. You can use this for a lot of problems in your life. Be it failing a test and thinking you'll never pass or being bullied and thinking people could never possibly like you. No matter what the problem is, you are not destined to hurt forever.

Another way we suffer is through inauthenticity, or in simpler words, not being true to ourselves. In a lot of cases, what hurts most is not pain, but the loss of identity that comes with it. A hypothetical king who loses his kingdom is not suffering a loss of physical things. How could he have experienced the whole kingdom anyway? He is suffering because he built up an inauthentic identity as a king. He viewed himself exactly as everyone else saw him, and he based his entire identity around that fact. He never valued himself as a person, as a unique being, just as a king. And, so, when he lost his kingdom, he lost everything.

What is authenticity? Well, it's made up of a load of different aspects. To be authentic is to interpret life through your own lens, to create your own meaning with which to interpret it. It means to love without limitations and to create freely. It means to be at home with yourself. It means knowing yourself and doing what you believe to be right. It means accepting what makes you different and exploring how that interacts with the world. It means making your own choices. It means loving yourself. It means not limiting or second-guessing yourself. Most simply, it means being yourself and making your own choices in spite of what others tell us. When we are inauthentic, we suffer a lot more than we would if we were authentic. To be authentic, we first have to know ourselves, and then we have to make choices that align with this self. Just doing what everyone wants you to do is not authentic, and it's a one way trip to suffering and dissatisfaction that many people don't realize they're taking until it's too late.

Find the Antidote

Whenever you find yourself feeling any sadness or powerlessness, give yourself 90 seconds to feel it and then stand up. Power-pose, jump up and down, or dance wildly to your favorite song. Remember that life is beautiful! Don't give your power away to any low feeling! This advice is from my own experience; I do it daily when I am feeling down and it works like magic. Try it—even if it doesn't work for you, it's important to be open to new strategies.

Take note of all the positive things in your life, and where they came from. Remember you have much more to look forward to! You may wake up with negative thoughts in your head but remember to look on the brightside. Do you have a family, friends, food, or a house? Any of these things are fantastic to have!

Think of how lucky it is that you're alive and write it down. Write down every time someone's been nice to you and everything that you're grateful for. Once you start writing it down, you'll be surprised by how much there is! No-one can take these positives away from you because they are yours to see and yours to find.

Ways to Be More Grateful

- **Don't be too picky:** Don't just save gratitude for the big things in life. Use it for the small things as well: The cookie you ate at lunchtime, the flower you see growing from the cracks in the sidewalk, the way the sunshine warms the back of your neck and the cold creates beautiful frost patterns on everything. The way your favorite show or book or movie makes you feel, and all the effort the creators put into it. Your friends' laughter, the butterflies and bees and moths when they come in the summer, your stuffed animal collection. Nothing's too small and insignificant to matter, there's nothing trivial in this universe. If all that existed in all space and time was a random chunk of rock floating forever, that would still be a miracle, because the very fact of existence itself is so strange and complex, so isn't it a double-triple-quadruple miracle that things that make you happy exist?

- **Find the positives in the negatives:** So, you failed a math test. Well, you can learn from your answers and try harder on the next one! Perhaps you can get a friend who's good at math to help you, or your teacher to go over the answers again. Every single challenge is a learning experience. Every single negative feeling is a part of truly being alive, truly living. Pain is awful, but it's proof you've survived this long, and you will survive more. And isn't that awesome? Feeling grateful about the bad things is well… hard. But it can help us immensely to see life through this lens!
- **Become a mindful person:** Use your senses more! Feel what's around you. Notice the little details and how cool and intricate everything is. Stop and smell the roses a bit more often. And practice taking time every day to specifically focus on what's around you, write it in your journal, and be grateful for it. Soon it will become a habit and a great one at that!
- **Focus on expression:** Sometimes simply feeling grateful isn't enough. We have to show it! Sometimes this can be through telling our friends and family how grateful we are for them. When we tell people how grateful we are, it's best to be specific. Instead of "thanks for being a great friend," you can say "thanks for always noticing when I need cheering up and asking if I'm ok, thanks for giving good advice about my crush and thanks for making me laugh when we talk about silly reality tv shows." Or whatever you're grateful for in your relationship with this person. Instead of saying "I love you mom," you could say "I love you for knowing my favorite dinner and making whenever you have the opportunity, I love you for

giving me a hug when I need it, and I love you for always helping me when I have a problem with my homework," or for whatever your guardian(s) does that you feel grateful for. But it doesn't just have to be those we are closest to. Even expressing gratitude to the waiter at a restaurant or a stranger who holds a door open for you is great!

- **Find those who love you:** Spend time with your loved ones. This will help you become more thankful for them, as well as becoming closer to them. It's a great way to become happier and more grateful. You'll also be able to practice your gratitude on them.
- **Keep a gratitude journal:** Write down the things you're grateful for every day. Remember that quality is better than quantity! Describing a few things in detail is better than listing a lot of things with no explanation.
- **Write a gratitude letter:** Think about something someone did for you that you haven't thanked them enough for. (Preferably someone you could meet in person). It doesn't matter how long ago it was. It could be a friend, relative, or teacher. Write a letter. Preferably make it less than one page. Start it with "Dear (name)." Grammar doesn't matter, what matters is you express genuine sentiment. Talk about how grateful you are for the act. Be specific! Then arrange to meet them. When you meet up, tell them you want to thank them and not to interrupt you until you're done, and then read out the letter to them. Let them keep the letter when they go away.
- **Go for a long walk:** Go on a walk, even just a short one if a long one won't do, every day for a week and notice all the beautiful things you see along the way.

Really savor them and try to figure out why you think they're so beautiful. Try to pick a different route each day, if you can, that way you don't become accustomed to your surroundings.
- **Imagine your life without these things:** Imagine your life without all the events, things and people you're grateful for. Imagine your life without the internet or without your best friend. In fact, try to give something you take for granted up for a week! Perhaps your smartphone, your morning cup of tea or coffee or your favorite hobby. Then, when you come back to this thing, you'll find you appreciate it so much more!
- **Focus on intention:** When someone gives you a gift, instead of focusing on the gift itself, focus on the intention. This person thought of you and went out of their way to give you something, no matter how big or small! Isn't it amazing that you have people that love you so much?
- **Remember the bad:** Sometimes it can work to remember how far you've come and how much you've gained. Perhaps you used to have trouble making friends in elementary school or middle school, but now you have a great group of friends who always make you laugh! Perhaps you struggled for two summers to find a part-time job, and this summer you were finally hired! Perhaps you used to argue with your siblings all the time, but now you get along better! Perhaps you used to fail a subject, but now you are passing it! I'm sure you can find some ways in which your life has improved since last year or even when you were a little kid. Maybe you simply have more independence. Whatever it is, it

can make us more grateful to visualize those bad times and compare it with how much better it is now.
- **Practice Naikan:** Naikan is a Japanese gratitude tradition, created by Buddhist monk Shinran Shonen back in the 13th century. It focuses on three questions: "what have I received from…?" "what have I given to…?" and "what difficulties have I caused…?" You can ask these questions about your relationship to the world in general, to communities, or to individual relationships. Meditate on them, truly think about it.
- **Be happy in other ways:** Being happy in other ways increases your gratitude, which then increases your happiness. It's a positive spiral! So go out, exercise, volunteer with causes that matter to you, spend time doing a hobby you love!

Positive Affirmations

What are affirmations, first of all? Affirmations are positive thoughts repeated in order to make you believe them more. It's often said you are what you think. If you believe you are doomed to fail, you will be. However, if you think you're in charge of your own success, you're more likely to achieve it. Affirmations are extremely helpful, and many people use them in daily life. They can help you in so many areas! They have been shown in scientific studies to reduce stress, make you more likely to eat healthier, improve grades, ruminate on events less, and feel less threatened by criticism! When someone criticizes you in one area of your life, you may get defensive. However, affirmations make you realize that the part they criticized you on isn't your whole self or even the most important part. It helps you put everything into perspective! Not only are you less hurt, but you're more likely to listen to the criticism and take action if the criticism is genuine. Affirmations also make you optimistic and resilient, because of that fact.

Here are some tips about affirmations:

- Affirmations work best when they're rooted in what values we hold dear. For example, if succeeding at school isn't something you really value in yourself then "I am a good student and will get all As" probably isn't the best affirmation. Instead, think about what you do care about within yourself. Are you a good friend, daughter, or sister? Do you work hard at a particular sport or hobby? Are you always as kind as you can be to strangers? What things are important to you and in what ways do you embody them or want to embody them in your life?

- Don't focus them all on the one value either. Remember you are multifaceted and complex, and in order for self-affirmations to work, you have to know that!
- Writing your affirmations in your journal, or on sticky notes somewhere you can see them on your wall, is a great idea! You can also say them in front of the mirror. Both of these techniques help the affirmations stick in your head!
- Affirmations can be said up to three to five times a day.
- Meditating with your affirmations is a great idea, just like we did with the Ultimate Success Mantra in Chapter 2.
- Some people use the words 'affirmation', 'incantation' and 'mantra' interchangeably. There is in fact a difference. Mantras tend to be shorter and to focus on the effect the sound produces rather than the meaning of the phrase (the soundwaves of the sacred Hindu mantra 'Om,' for example, are scientifically proven to have an extremely positive calming effect on the mind and body). They are also usually religious or spiritual, though they can be used in secular contexts. Incantations and affirmations are longer, focus more on the meaning of the words and are less likely to have religious connotations.
- An example of a type of affirmation is a healing affirmation. This was popularized by Louise Hay who was diagnosed with irreversible cervical cancer back in the 1970s after experiencing all sorts of abuse and still lived into her nineties. She credits her longevity to her health affirmations. Whether or not you're sick, you can try out these health mantras!

"My mind and body are in perfect balance. I am a harmonious being," or "Wellness is the natural state of my body. I believe in perfect health."
- Positive affirmations require practice and daily repetition if you want to make an actual difference. They aren't magic words!

Here are some affirmations you can use. Pick the ones that mean something to you.

- I am enough.
- The more I love myself, the more others will like me.
- Sometimes I make mistakes, and I will forgive myself for them like I forgive others.
- I deserve to focus on myself.
- My self-worth comes from within, and not from others' approval.
- I am a human being, complex and whole. I am no better nor worse than that.
- I am smart, but I don't know everything, and that's okay.
- I am secure in myself and my surroundings.
- It's okay to feel pain. That's just a part of being alive.
- It's okay if I'm not in control of everything all the time.
- My thoughts and feelings matter.
- My actions will become habits, so I'll do the right thing.
- So many people love and care about me.
- I can't be liked by everyone all the time, that's simply not possible.
- Nothing in this universe is perfect, so I don't have to be.

- I am grateful for my friends and family.
- I am working to be the best version of me possible.
- I have the power to overcome any challenges life throws my way.
- I am choosing, not waiting to be chosen.
- Every day I become stronger and kinder.
- I will accept the things I can't change.
- I learn from my mistakes, and it's okay that I make them.
- I both love and am loved unconditionally. Love isn't something that has to be earned.
- My own growth is important, and I will focus on it.
- I am happy without overworking.
- I no longer fear failure.
- I am more than my emotions.
- I can create a beautiful reality instead of just withdrawing into a beautiful fantasy.
- Others can understand me if I let them.
- I am confident and competent.
- I savor living life in the moment.
- I take action instead of complaining about things.
- I trust my instincts.
- I can be satisfied without people or things in my life.
- I am focused and complete projects.
- I am allowed to be vulnerable.
- I will stand up for others.
- The choices I make make my reality.
- I act instead of procrastinating.
- I take good care of my body.
- I am not defined by my grades.
- I am kind to myself.
- I am magical in my uniqueness.
- I am motivated to do better.

If you do what you've always done, you'll get what you've always gotten

— JESSIE POTTER

Think About the Positives

Whenever we come up against challenges, they sap a smidgeon of our faith. Eventually, without properly taking care of your mental wellbeing, you're going to find pessimism creeping in. We can help fight this with positive thinking and mindfulness. Positive thinking is when we see the good in life and we are optimistic about the future. It contributes to our overall well-being, increases our immunity, and makes us more resilient and less stressed. It won't fix every problem in life, but it will certainly make you deal with them better. Pessimism is far from realism. In fact, it's just another coping strategy. If you believe that everything will go wrong before it even happens, you don't have to try! Instead, focus on taking the good out of bad situations. Focus on facing challenges head on. Focus on believing you can do it!

Having positive energy is more than just thoughts. It's about belief! It's about believing that there truly is good in the world. That joy, love, and fulfillment exist both within you already and everywhere in the world around you. That the future is clay, and you are a sculptress with hands ready, about to create something so beautiful it will strike wonder into the hearts of the harshest critics. Despite all the hardships, the challenges, the pain, you will bounce back with a grin on your face, screaming "come at me world!" So, how do we encourage positive thinking in our lives?

We need to radiate happiness. What small things make you content? Be it listening to your favorite playlist, playing soccer with your team, or writing stories, treat yourself to those things and try to capture the happiness that you feel in that moment. Ask the people around you what makes them happy, and listen to them talk about it, or if it's an activity, ask if you can try it with them! Engaging in the happiness of others is very likely to make you more happy. Make sure you approach the situation with an open mindset and are willing to learn!

Create a space in your mind, a safe sanctuary of joy. Think of a memory, a moment, or a place that will really lighten your spirits. Be it cooking with your grandmother, running, or a great joke that always makes you laugh, capture it and make it a happy place in your mind you can go to. Remind yourself that, no matter what, you'll always be capable of producing that happiness.

One surefire way of *not* being happy and positive is comparing yourself to others. You are who you are. It doesn't matter if you're struggling at school while other students—especially your siblings—are getting As. It doesn't matter if you see your classmates at a party on social media while you remain home alone. It does matter that you accept yourself. Not everyone is good at everything, and you don't have to be 'perfect' to be complete. The world is filled with people, and each one is entirely unique. Being like everyone else is boring and overrated. Plus, not everyone is as happy and successful as they seem on social media, or even in real life. You often don't get the full story. So don't fall down the compare-and-despair rabbit hole! Practice accepting yourself as often as you can.

Practice self-love! Take regular breaks from school and work. Sleep well, eat well, and exercise well. Become happy in your own company. Write in your journal all the things you like about yourself. Talk aloud to yourself, telling yourself everything will work out okay in the end. Because it will. And saying them aloud will reinforce this truth.

Don't block out all negative thoughts. Some can be beneficial for us. Like I said about the movie *Inside Out* in the beginning, all emotions serve their purpose to keep you safe and happy. It's unhealthy to just ignore them. Instead, acknowledge the thoughts, and remember it doesn't define anything. Then, reframe them more realistically. Avoid negative words and all-or-nothing thinking. It's okay to feel bad. These things happen.

Autosuggestion is a trick you can try. It's defined by Merriam-Webster as "an influencing on one's own attitudes, behavior, or physical condition by mental processes other than conscious thought." Basically, that means you repeat positive words and phrases in order to change your perception, and thus your reality. This often has amazing results! Think of a goal, and phrase it as an "I choose…" phrase. For example, "I choose to increase my grade in biology" or "I choose to make new friends. Then repeat this phrase. You can meditate on it too, repeat it aloud, play it back to yourself while you sleep, or write it somewhere you'll see it every day. This is not just magic or wishful thinking. You're just replacing thoughts you already have on the topic. Subconsciously, you're probably thinking "I won't ever increase my grades in biology" or "I could never make new friends." This is impacting your performance in these areas! Autosuggestion is replacing these phrases with new better ones.

Find a mentor, someone you look up to. It can be an older relative, teacher, or even one of your parents. It's important to have one good adult you can trust and look up to. Try also to think of people you are inspired by, be it famous actors, writers, scientists, activists, or sportspeople. What do you find inspirational in these people? What can you learn from them? What can they tell you about who you want to be?

You should also consider, if it's possible, getting a life coach or therapist, or even just talking to your school guidance counselor. These people will get to know you, your challenges and blindspots, and hold you accountable to your goals of self-improvement!

It's important to surround yourself with support. Surround yourself with people who care about you, give you courage and accept you for who you are. If you have trouble finding good friends, try joining a club of something you're interested in, so you can meet people who have things in common with you. Humans are social creatures, even though it might not feel like it sometimes, so it's important to have those who love you. For some people, it may seem near impossible right now, but I promise you can be loved and accepted for who you are.

7

LET'S GET PRACTICAL!

THE ART OF EXERCISE

What Exercise Can Do For You

Listen, I don't want to sound like your PE teacher or your mother. But there are *reasons* everyone promotes exercise, and it's not just to annoy you. Exercise is extremely beneficial to both your body and mind. Let's take a look at some of the benefits, shall we?

- Exercise reduces your risk of developing depression or even just a sad mood. If you do have depression, it can alleviate the severity of the symptoms.
- It causes you to be more likely to perform better in school.
- It improves your memory, processing speed, and executive function—even if you have a disorder that affects those things.

- It reduces your chance of your memory deteriorating as you get older.
- It helps you sleep better, both in the short term and the long term.
- It can alleviate symptoms of stress and anxiety.
- It reduces your chance of developing many physical ailments, including cancers and heart diseases.
- It gives you stronger bones and muscles.
- It's associated with high overall life satisfaction.
- It produces more endorphins or "happy chemicals" in your brain, which improves your mood.
- It increases brain power.
- It makes your skin 'glow.'
- It can increase your energy levels.
- It can reduce pain.
- It increases self-esteem.
- It can be fun and social!

Personally, I love running! It's like therapy for me; it relaxes me, and I always find myself more creative afterward. My mind gets clear, and I begin to see things from a more rational perspective. I become very resourceful and start working towards a rational and creative solution.

If you don't exercise already, starting small and slowly increasing the amount of exercise you do is extremely important. Seven hours a week, once a day, is what's recommended for those aged eighteen and under, but if you start with that right away, you will end up overwhelmed and overworked, and it might put you off exercise altogether! Start off doing one or two hours a week and slowly increase it. Make sure it's something you enjoy, but don't knock anything until you've tried it. You might find fun in the most unusual of places. Perhaps your school or community has sports clubs you could join! Be it soccer, martial arts, dance, or athletics, you're sure to find something that piques your interest! If you feel nervous about it, invite a friend to come with you. Or, you could exercise at home! There are a ton of easy workout videos that don't require much equipment on YouTube that you could try following, or you could play outside with your younger siblings, relatives, or neighbors. The possibilities are endless. It all starts with physiology—start your routine with a power pose!

Even something as small as walking or cycling to school can make a huge difference! Recent research indicates that those of us who do as little as 10 minutes a day, or once a week, are significantly happier than those who don't exercise at all. Exercise can also help us get into a beautiful state of mind. This state is full of calmness, gratitude, clarity, spontaneity, and compassion. This can help us approach solutions quicker, especially if a beautiful state is our default or "home" state. Our quality of life is the quality of where we live emotionally.

THE KEY IS PROPER SLEEP

What This Can Do For You

Sleep is extremely important for both our physical health and our mental wellbeing. Without it, we become irritable, anxious, unstable, forgetful, and inattentive. Our school work tends to suffer and we are at higher risk of accidents because we have difficulty concentrating. We experience severe distress more frequently, and we have reduced immunity, putting us at higher risk for many damaging physical ailments. But, despite this, 35% of American adults don't get enough sleep per night. It's important to remember a teenager needs more sleep than an adult does, 8–10 hours a night.

The benefits of sleep are seemingly endless. Let's first talk about learning. Of course, learning at school is important, but this doesn't just refer to that. Learning more about your hobbies, learning more about your friends, learning anything about the world around you—these are all things that we do every day, and they affect our lives a lot. There are two reasons why sleep impacts learning and memory. The first is, as I said before, sleep deprivation leads to worse concentration which leads to less learning. The second is that sleep has a very important role in sticking information we learn while awake into our brain. So you're definitely not going to learn a lot when you're tired. Maybe it's a better idea to go to bed and finish studying for that test early tomorrow morning, instead of cramming all night!

Sleep also has a massive impact on your emotional state. Even partial sleep deprivation leads to one becoming sad, angry, and mentally drained a lot more often. You probably know this already—after a night of poor sleep, it's very likely that the people around you will notice how grumpy you are! But it goes even deeper than that. People who struggle with sleep are significantly more likely to develop depression and anxiety disorders. One study showed that those with insomnia are 5 times more likely to develop depression and *20 times* more likely to develop anxiety. These in turn can have a massive impact on your sleep.

Remember how we talked about exercise earlier in this chapter? Well, sleep influences exercise as well. People who experience poor sleep are less likely to exercise, both in the long term and the short term. Just one night of poor sleep can make you less likely to exercise the next day and on top of that, poor sleep one year can lead to less exercising in up to 5 years. Better sleep also leads to better performance in athletes and fewer injuries.

A way to improve your sleep is to establish a proper sleep routine. Go to bed at the same time every night and wake up at the same time every morning. Limit both caffeine and screen time before bed. Make your bed more comfortable. Eat enough, drink enough water, and exercise regularly—though, don't do any of these things before bed. Get more light during the day and less at night. Do something comforting before bed, like reading, listening to calming music, or meditation. Go to sleep when you're really tired and don't take naps too close to bedtime. You don't have to do all of these things, but try them out and see which of them suits you.

VOLUNTEER IN THE COMMUNITY

The Power of Volunteering

It's always great to do something good for those around you, but did you know that volunteering with a local organization has benefits not only for your community but for yourself as well? Volunteering can lower stress and make you more active, giving you better health. It develops your skills and gives you a sense of purpose. It improves your self-esteem, reduces your risk of depression, and helps you socialize and meet new people. It stimulates your brain, improves problem-solving and social skills, and it can even help you with career experience—it looks very good on a resumé!

Research organizations near you that you could volunteer for. Make sure you pick something you're interested in! If there aren't any organizations near you, there are often things you could do online. You could even set up your own group—perhaps you and some friends could pick up litter in your neighborhood or perform random acts of kindness. If you can, try volunteering for just one day first to see if you like the organization. Any acts of kindness are better than none at all, and so it doesn't have to take a lot of time out of your schedule or require a long-term commitment. Notice how your mood improves while you're doing it, too.

FIND YOUR OPPORTUNITIES

The Power of Opportunities

What separates the successful from the unsuccessful people? Of course, luck and circumstance play a part. So do motivation, education, and passion. But one of the main differences is that successful people recognize how to seize opportunities when they appear. They know how to make the best out of what they're given. They find the sweetness in the situation, extract it, and use it to make lemonade out of life's infamous lemons. For those who seek, opportunities abound.

It's impossible to know when opportunities will come and why, but it is possible to be prepared. The most important part of being prepared is knowing what you want and knowing what will get you closer to that goal. It's important to be in a beautiful state of mind in order to see the opportunity in situations. It's up to you to choose to see the power that every opportunity brings.

Try to see the lesson in everything. You can grow from every situation, no matter how bad it may seem. It will find its place in your story eventually. Let yourself grow into the person you were meant to be. Focus on your unique abilities, your unique opportunities, and what you can do with them to produce something awe-inspiring.

Change Your Life Towards Opportunity

> *If we could change ourselves, the tendencies in the world would also change.*
>
> — MOHANDAS GANDHI

If we want to see change, we have to change ourselves. If you want opportunities, go out and find them! Research, ask questions, volunteer for projects! Take control! Opportunity doesn't just come knocking on your door. You're not a backseat passenger in your own life. You're not in some dress rehearsal waiting for real life to begin. This is your life. *This is it.* All these moments are you, living. So, make them something great! Make your life into something *you* are proud of, whatever that means. Take steps, make plans, envision something good! Making changes might make you uncomfortable, but that's okay. Sometimes, when we grow, we get growing pains. You'll become accustomed to the newness of it.

Ask the Right Questions:

- How can I make this happen?
- What can I control?
- What can I be grateful for?
- What is another way to look at this and find a solution?
- How can I be better?
- How can I get more resourceful?

Take Charge of Your Own Future

Write down everything you want, no matter how big or small. Don't miss a single thing! Ask yourself, "Which of these can I work towards right now?" Focus on one thing; prioritize. Make sure it's something *you* want and you're using *your* skills to achieve it. It's important to be authentic in what you're doing. The world is full of distractions! It's less stressful and more effective to focus on one project at a time. You can worry about the next project *after* this one is done.

Or better still, don't worry at all. Stop to smell the roses. You really will burn out trying to do everything fast. It's so very important that you go at your own pace. Whatever that pace is, it doesn't matter. Sometimes, slow and steady really does win the race—because life is a marathon, not a sprint. Be grateful for the here and now, for every opportunity you have.

QUICK AND EFFECTIVE HOMEWORK

Here's an example of a day in the life of someone practicing positive thinking, affirmations, and gratitude! Set up to 3 alarms on your phone daily, each with a different song you love and an empowering quote.

If you get up at 7:00 a.m., set an alarm for 7:30 a.m. when you're still a bit groggy and in need of motivation. Something to pump you up and energize you! Let your alarm blast an enthusiastic song, with an affirmation like, "I start everyday with enthusiasm, optimism, and love!"

By lunchtime, you're sleepy, bored and your attention span is diminished. That's when you set your alarm with another pump-me-up song, when you know you're on recess— and if your school allows it of course! This time, use a quote like, "You know you got this!" to put yourself back into the positive mindset.

The first thing you do when you get home from school is to tell your parents or loved ones the good things that happened to you today. Whatever that may be, whether the bus driver waited for you, your teacher gave you a compliment or you read a beautiful quote that made you reflect on it. It might be hard to see all the good things at first, but it will become easier once you do this every day. No exceptions. No complaints. Make it a daily habit!

Then, after dinner, it may be time to add some gratitude to your phone alarm. Think to yourself, "I'm so grateful for my family, the great meal I just had, and that I'm home. I'm grateful that I can attend school; I'm grateful that I'm healthy. I'm so grateful for the time spent with my grandparents," or whatever you're grateful for in your life. Make sure you listen to a beautiful song that makes you feel grateful to go along with it!

Listen to motivational speakers on YouTube. My recommendations are Tony Robbins, Jim Rhone, Joe Dispenza, Wayne Dyer, and *The Secret* documentary. These will all help you to boost your positive mindset!

Here's another writing challenge for your journal—to imagine your goal. Imagine today that you receive a letter. It's from yourself, 10 years in the future! What would you like it to say? What things, great or small, will you have accomplished? What does your life look like? What advice would you give yourself? Write it all down!

Writing it down in a journal is a great therapist. You can admit so much to a journal and not be in fear that it will judge you or not understand you.

— MY COUSIN ANCUȚA

CONCLUSION (CHECK THE PAGE AFTER)

I have faith that you're leaving this book more powerful and courageous. I hope what you learned about the powers of journaling stays with you throughout your teenage years and well beyond. I have faith that whatever challenges come your way you can face them with a confident smile on your face.

Your future is yours to plan, to take control of. Every decision you make is entirely yours. Every decision you make is important, but it isn't the end of the world. You are resilient. You can forgive and be forgiven. You can find your way again, no matter what. You'll bounce back with such enthusiasm because you have a kernel of light, of hope, of love, determination, and courage buried deep inside you, and, no matter what, it can't be taken away. No matter what others say or expect from you, no matter what that insecure voice says, you will always have the ability to look upon the world from a positive mindset. Through loss, through pain, through heartbreak, may you stand strong and confident and may your strength be like a beacon to those you love.

You are you and will never be anyone else. You're an entirely unique beauty, an undeniable work of art occupying space in the universe. A group of atoms somehow taken control of by a sentient force, capable of so much good. And, my goodness, isn't that beautiful? May you never forget that beauty. May you never forget how rare it is that you exist. How rare it is that you can love yourself and others. And may you love yourself and others without limitations, and love others without them too.

May you be happy and healthy in every aspect of the word. May you feel alright, may you exercise right and sleep right, may you meditate and affirm right. May you know how you should be treated and never allow anyone to treat you otherwise. May your default state be a beautiful one. May you reach your zone of genius and contribute all of your talents to the world. May you know when you are right and apologize when you are wrong.

May you be grateful for everything. The world around you is undeniably full of things to be grateful for, and the more you try, the easier it becomes, even at the hardest time. Grow from every challenge you face. At the end of the day, may you have a million stories to tell, and may you find a moral in all of them. May Plutchik's Wheel help you learn to bring language to the seemingly indescribable, the deep, and the mundane.

May you always ask the right questions. May the language you use create a beautiful world, inside and outside. May you plan and plan and plan. May you break out of your Upper Limit Problem. May you seize every opportunity. Your life is yours and yours alone, may you never ever forget that. May

CONCLUSION (CHECK THE PAGE AFTER) | 121

your thoughts, your language and your physiology make you confident and unstoppable.

I hope this book finds a place in your heart or in your subconscious. May you never forget what power you hold and how to unleash it. Your power, as a teenage girl, is unlimited, and with the right confidence, courage, mindset, and planning, you can and will take on the world. I believe in you. Time to believe in yourself.

The only person you are destined to become is the person you decide to be.

— RALPH WALDO EMERSON

Stay tuned for my next book and if you enjoyed this one, as an independent author filled with passion to share my knowledge and experience with others, I will appreciate it greatly if you could please leave me an honest review! See below:

Scan/Click here

I have created this gratitude and plan your day journal just for you, to guide you in creating an empowering life that you were meant to live:

If you want to share or post this book on social media, please use these:

#TeenageGirlPower
#Journaling
#Mindfulness
#GirlPower
#TakeBackYourPower
#StartNow
#EmpoweringYouth
#TeenageLife
#TeenageGirl
#BeKindToYourself
#ParentingTeenagers
#WomenEmpoweringWomen

REFERENCES

5 Options Radio Collective. (2018, February 25). 5 reasons why you may be creating drama in your life without even realizing it. The 5 Options. https://www.the5options.com/blog-articles/2018/2/26/5-reasons-why-you-may-be-creating-drama

Adler, L. (2021, March 24). How Exercise Affects Sleep. Sleep.org. https://www.sleep.org/exercise-affects-sleep/

Ahlzen, R. (2020). Suffering, authenticity, and physician assisted suicide. Medicine, Health Care and Philosophy, 23, 353–359. https://doi.org/10.1007/s11019-019-09929-z

Ajay Anil Gurjar, Ladhake, S. A., & Thakare, A. P. (2009). Analysis Of Acoustic of " OM " Chant To Study It's Effect on Nervous System. IJCSNS International Journal of Computer Science and Network Security, 9(1). http://paper.ijcsns.org/07_book/200901/20090151.pdf

Almeida, C. M. O. de, & Malheiro, A. (2016). Sleep, immunity and shift workers: A review. Sleep Science, 9(3), 164–168. https://doi.org/10.1016/j.slsci.2016.10.007

Armenta, C. N., Fritz, M. M., & Lyubomirsky, S. (2016). Functions of Positive Emotions: Gratitude as a Motivator of Self-Improvement and Positive Change. Emotion Review, 9(3). https://doi.org/10.1177/1754073916669596

Assistant Secretary for Public Affairs (ASPA. (2019, September 24). Who Is at Risk. StopBullying.gov; StopBullying.gov. https://www.stopbullying.gov/bullying/at-risk

Atkins, M. (2013, October 8). 50 First Strength Based Questions. Changed Lives New Journeys. https://www.changedlivesnewjourneys.com/50-first-strength-based-questions/

Bahra, M. (2021, April 7). Emotional Contagion — Why You Must Be Careful Who You Surround Yourself With. Medium. https://medium.com/game-of-self/emotional-contagion-why-you-must-be-careful-who-you-surround-yourself-with-a8e2201988c0

Baragona, L. (2018, February 9). 8 signs that prove you're not ready for a relationship. Insider. https://www.insider.com/am-i-ready-for-a-relationship-2018-2

Barbara. (n.d.). A Big Leap Shortcut | Unity of Port Richey. Www.unityportrichey.org. Retrieved July 28, 2021, from https://www.unityportrichey.org/big-leap-shortcut

Barnes, H. (2020). Suffering Lies in Your Perception of the Fact and Not the Fact Itself. Harrisonbarnes.com. https://www.harrisonbarnes.com/suffering-lies-in-your-perception-of-the-fact-and-not-the-fact-itself/amp/

Beckes, L., Coan, J. A., & Hasselmo, K. (2012). Familiarity promotes the blurring of self and other in the neural representation of threat. Social Cognitive and Affective Neuroscience, 8(6), 670–677. https://doi.org/10.1093/scan/nss046

Benthal, E. (2020, February 16). Life is unpredictable, but how we respond to life is within our control. RiverheadLOCAL. https://riverheadlocal.com/2020/02/16/life-is-unpredictable-but-how-we-respond-to-life-is-within-our-control/

Bergland, C. (2016, January 10). Your Brain Can Be Trained to Self-Regulate Negative Thinking. Psychology Today. https://www.psychologytoday.com/us/blog/the-athletes-way/201601/your-brain-can-be-trained-self-regulate-negative-thinking

Berkeley Centre of Science for The Greater Good. (2019). Gratitude Definition | What Is Gratitude. Greater Good. https://greatergood.berkeley.edu/topic/gratitude/definition

Berkeley Centre of Science for the Greater Good. (n.d.). Forgiveness Definition | What Is Forgiveness. Greater Good. Retrieved August 3, 2021, from https://greatergood.berkeley.edu/topic/forgiveness/definition#why-practice-forgiveness

Berlinsky-Schine, L. (n.d.). How to Check In With Yourself (in 2 Minutes or Less) Using an Emotion Wheel. Fairygodboss.com. Retrieved July 25, 2021, from https://fairygodboss.com/career-topics/emotion-wheel#

Birgit Online. (2014, July). Clear and Brief Emotions. Brigit Online. http://www.br-online.de/jugend/izi/english/publication/televizion/27_2014_E/Kinateder.pdf

Booth, A. L. (2003). We are the Land: Native American Views of Nature. Science across Cultures: The History of Non-Western Science, 329–349. https://doi.org/10.1007/978-94-017-0149-5_17

Boyes, A. (2015). 51 Signs of an Unhealthy Relationship. Psychology Today. https://www.psychologytoday.com/us/blog/in-practice/201502/51-signs-unhealthy-relationship

Brame, G. (2019, February 20). If You're Not True to Yourself, No One Else Will Be. Dr. Gloria Brame. https://www.gloriabrame.com/if-youre-not-true-to-yourself-no-one-else-will-be/

Braxton-Davis, P. (2010). The Social Psychology of Love and Attraction. McNair Scholars Journal, 14(2). https://scholarworks.gvsu.edu/cgi/viewcontent.cgi?article=1235&context=mcnair

Breaux, K. (2020, July 8). Healing Is Not Linear, So Don't Rush The Process. Thought Catalog. https://thoughtcatalog.com/kelsey-breaux/2020/07/healing-is-not-linear-so-dont-rush-the-process/

Browne, S. (2020, September 1). How to Appreciate Life More and Be Grateful. Lifehack. https://www.lifehack.org/885124/appreciate-life

Cambridge. (n.d.). come to terms with sth. Dictionary.cambridge.org. Retrieved July 25, 2021, from https://dictionary.cambridge.org/dictionary/english/come-to-terms-with-sth

Carmody, B. (2015, December 12). Tony Robbins Shares 5 Words That Change Everything. Inc.com. https://www.inc.com/bill-carmody/tony-robbins-shares-5-words-that-change-everything.html

Cavanaugh, J. (2016, July 19). You Can't Rush Your Healing. The Odyssey Online. https://www.theodysseyonline.com/you-cant-rush-your-healing

Centralised Counselling at MIT. (2010). Introduction to Problem Solving Skills | CCMIT. Mit.edu. https://ccmit.mit.edu/problem-solving/

Centre for Disease Control. (2016, January 1). 1 in 3 adults don't get enough sleep. CDC. https://www.cdc.gov/media/releases/2016/p0215-enough-sleep.html

Cherry, K. (2012, March 5). Benefits of Positive Thinking for Body and Mind. Verywell Mind; Verywellmind. https://www.verywellmind.com/benefits-of-positive-thinking-2794767

Cherry, K. (2019). The 6 Types of Basic Emotions and Their Effect on Human Behavior (S. Gans, Ed.). Verywell Mind. https://www.verywellmind.com/an-overview-of-the-types-of-emotions-4163976

Cherry, K. (2021, February 17). How to forgive yourself. Verywell Mind. https://www.verywellmind.com/how-to-forgive-yourself-4583819

Collins Thesaurus of the English Language. (2002). state of mind. TheFreeDictionary.com. https://www.thefreedictionary.com/state+of+mind

Conner, C. (2014, September 20). Teen Entrepreneur Megan Grassell Used Her Frustration To Fuel A Business. Forbes. https://www.forbes.com/sites/cherylsnappconner/2014/09/20/teen-entrepreneur-megan-grassell-used-her-frustration-to-fuel-a-business/

Crawford, K. (2021, April 5). Self-Love is a Radical Act. Hercampus.com. https://www.hercampus.com/school/delaware/self-love-radical-act/

Critcher, C. R., & Dunning, D. (2014). Self-Affirmations Provide a Broader Perspective on Self-Threat. Personality and Social Psychology Bulletin, 41(1), 3–18. https://doi.org/10.1177/0146167214554956

Cuddy, A. J. C., Wilmuth, C. A., & Carney, D. R. (2012). The Benefit of Power Posing Before a High-Stakes Social Evaluation. https://dash.harvard.edu/bitstream/handle/1/9547823/13-027.pdf?sequence%3D1

CYACYL New York, & Hendricks, G. (2011). Interview with Gay Hendricks. Www.youtube.com. https://www.youtube.com/watch?v=Vqterautik0&t=14s

David, D., Cristea, I., & Hofmann, S. G. (2018). Why Cognitive Behavioral Therapy Is the Current Gold Standard of Psychotherapy. Frontiers in Psychiatry, 9(4). https://doi.org/10.3389/fpsyt.2018.00004

Division of Sleep Medicine at Harvard Medical School. (2007, December 18). Sleep, Learning, and Memory | Healthy Sleep. Healthysleep.med.harvard.edu. https://healthysleep.med.harvard.edu/healthy/matters/benefits-of-sleep/learning-memory

Division of Sleep Medicine at Harvard Medical School. (2008a, December 12). Adopt Good Sleep Habits | Need Sleep. Healthysleep.med.harvard.edu. https://healthysleep.med.harvard.edu/need-sleep/what-can-you-do/good-sleep-habits

Division of Sleep Medicine at Harvard Medical School. (2008b, December 15). Sleep and Mood | Need Sleep. Healthysleep.med.harvard.edu. https://healthysleep.med.harvard.edu/need-sleep/whats-in-it-for-you/mood

Division of Sleep Medicine at Harvard Medicine School. (2007, December 18). Why Do We Sleep, Anyway? | Healthy Sleep. Healthysleep.med.harvard.edu. https://healthysleep.med.harvard.edu/healthy/matters/benefits-of-sleep/why-do-we-sleep

Donaldson, M. (2017). Plutchik's Wheel of Emotions - 2017 Update. http://www.uvm.edu/~mjk/013%20Intro%20to%20Wildlife%20Tracking/Plutchik%27s%20Wheel%20of%20Emotions%20-%202017%20Update%20_%20Six%20Seconds.pdf

Dunford, N. (2016, March 14). 11 Signs Your Business Has A Serious Upper Limit Problem. IttyBiz. https://ittybiz.com/upper-limit-problem/

Emmons, R. (2010, November 17). 10 Ways to Become More Grateful. Greater Good. https://greatergood.berkeley.edu/article/item/ten_ways_to_become_more_grateful1/

Emmons, R. A. (2010). Why Gratitude Is Good. Greater Good. https://greatergood.berkeley.edu/article/item/why_gratitude_is_good

Encyclopedia Britannica. (n.d.). Mantra | Buddhism and Hinduism. Encyclopedia Britannica. https://www.britannica.com/topic/mantra

Engel, B. (2017, June 1). Healing Your Shame and Guilt Through Self-Forgiveness. Psychology Today. https://www.psychologytoday.com/us/blog/the-compassion-chronicles/

201706/healing-your-shame-and-guilt-through-self-forgiveness

Fischer, W. (2021, May 15). How to meditate: A beginner's guide to meditation and mindfulness. Insider. https://www.insider.com/how-to-meditate

Gadd, A. (2019, July 13). Enneagram Type Specific Affirmations. Enneagrams 9 Paths. https://enneagrams9paths.com/enneagram-type-specific-affirmations/

Gordon, S. (2021, July 16). 7 Ways to Feel More Courageous. Verywell Mind. https://www.verywellmind.com/7-ways-to-feel-more-courageous-5089058

Graham, L. (2014, May 13). How to Overcome Barriers to Forgiveness (Berkeley Centre of Science for the Greater Good, Ed.). Greater Good. https://greatergood.berkeley.edu/article/item/overcome_barriers_forgiveness

Grassel, M. (n.d.). Megan's Story. Yellowberry. Retrieved July 24, 2021, from https://www.yellowberrycompany.com/pages/megans-story

Greater Good In Action. (n.d.-a). Gratitude Journal (Greater Good in Action). Ggia.berkeley.edu. Retrieved August 6, 2021, from https://ggia.berkeley.edu/practice/gratitude_journal?_ga=2.235205442.279249226.1628254341-98726842.1627491214

Greater Good In Action. (n.d.-b). Gratitude Letter (Greater Good in Action). Ggia.berkeley.edu. Retrieved August 6, 2021, from https://ggia.berkeley.edu/practice/gratitude_letter?_ga=2.208598097.279249226.1628254341-98726842.1627491214

Greater Good In Action. (n.d.-c). Savoring Walk (Greater Good in Action). Ggia.berkeley.edu. Retrieved August 6, 2021, from https://ggia.berkeley.edu/practice/savoring_walk?_ga=2.133503053.279249226.1628254341-98726842.1627491214

Gregersen, H., & Team Tony. (2018, November 14). Are you asking yourself the right questions? Tonyrobbins.com. https://www.tonyrobbins.com/mind-meaning/are-you-asking-yourself-the-right-questions/

Gross, E. L. (2017, April 17). How Yellowberry Is Changing The Bra Industry For Pre-Teens. Forbes. https://www.forbes.com/sites/elanagross/2017/04/17/how-yellowberry-is-changing-the-bra-industry-for-pre-teens/

Hailey, J. (n.d.). Whip It (2009) - IMDb. Www.imdb.com. Retrieved July 24, 2021, from https://www.imdb.com/title/tt1172233/?ref_=tt_rvi_tt_i_2

Hallowell, E. H. (2016). Fighting Life's "What Ifs." Psychology Today. https://www.psychologytoday.com/us/articles/199711/fighting-lifes-what-ifs

Hamlat, S. (2020). Autosuggestion: Theory and Practice. American Journal of Sciences and Engineering Research Www.iarjournals.com, 63(5),. https://iarjournals.com/upload/356369.pdf

Harvard Health Publishing. (2019, May). The power of forgiveness - Harvard Health. Harvard Health; Harvard Health. https://www.health.harvard.edu/mind-and-mood/the-power-of-forgiveness

Hazelden Betty Ford Foundation. (2020, August 5). Making Amends in Your Steps to Recovery. Www.hazeldenbettyford.org. https://www.hazeldenbettyford.org/articles/making-amends-addiction-recovery

Hendricks, G. (2009, October). No Limits.... More Happiness and Success Than You Thought Possible. Experience Life. https://www.dropbox.com/s/ki0mormq7dd90s1/No%20Limits%21%2010-6-09_Gay_Article_Experience_Life_Mag.pdf?dl=0

Hendricks, G. (2010). The big leap : conquer your hidden fear and take life to the next level. Harpercollins.

Hill, D. (2017, April 5). 20 Simple Ways to Bring Positive Energy into Life Right Now. Lifehack. https://www.lifehack.org/569466/how-regain-your-positive-energy-when-things-are-getting-tough

Hurd, S. (2019, February 27). Why Some People Love Drama and Conflict (and How to Deal with Them) - Learning Mind. Www.learning-Mind.com. https://www.learning-mind.com/people-love-drama-conflict/

A quote by Anthony Robbins. (n.d.). Www.goodreads.com. Retrieved August 9, 2021, from https://www.goodreads.com/quotes/179394-focus-equals-feeling

Bruce Lee Quotes: Courage is not the absence of fear,.... (1 C.E., November 30). Famous Inspirational Quotes & Sayings. https://www.inspirationalstories.com/quotes/bruce-lee-courage-is-not-the-absence-of-fear/

Confidence | Psychology Today. (2019). Psychology Today. https://www.psychologytoday.com/us/basics/confidence

Gimme Shelter (2014). (n.d.). Tvtropes.org. Retrieved July 24, 2021, from https://tvtropes.org/pmwiki/pmwiki.php/Film/GimmeShelter2014

Instructables, & zinrath. (2018, February 27). How to Plan Effectively. Instructables; Instructables. https://www.instructables.com/How-to-Plan-Effectively/

JDcarlu. (2015, March 24). 7 tips to give the right advice. Medium. https://medium.com/startup-frontier/7-tips-to-give-the-right-advice-c4ee1cf6b345

Joan, R. (2019, March 5). 5 Daily Actions to Build Your Confidence | Psychology Today. Www.psychologytoday.com. https://www.psychologytoday.com/us/blog/emotional-mastery/201903/5-daily-actions-build-your-confidence

Karimova, H. (2017, December 24). The Emotion Wheel: What It Is and How to Use It [+PDF]. PositivePsychology.com. https://positivepsychology.com/emotion-wheel/

Kelly, M. (2013, April 6). Everybody is a Genius. But If You Judge a Fish by Its Ability to Climb a Tree, It Will Live Its Whole Life Believing that It is Stupid – Quote Investigator. Quoteinvestigator.com. https://quoteinvestigator.com/2013/04/06/fish-climb/

Kerendian, D. (2016, August 10). Mantras vs. Affirmations: What's the Difference? Institute for Integrative Nutrition. https://www.integrativenutrition.com/blog/2016/08/mantras-vs-affirmations-what-s-the-difference

Key, K. (2015). You Can't Rush Grief. Psychology Today. https://www.psychologytoday.com/us/blog/counseling-keys/201512/you-cant-rush-grief

KidsHealth. (2017). Am I in a Healthy Relationship? (for Teens) - KidsHealth. Kidshealth.org. https://kidshealth.org/en/teens/healthy-relationship.html

Kim, J. (2016, November 22). Do Men Really Get Over Breakups Faster Than Women? Psychology Today. https://www.psychologytoday.com/us/blog/valley-girl-brain/201611/do-men-really-get-over-breakups-faster-women

Koifman, N. (2015, August 20). Your Destiny Is Determined by Your Decisions. HuffPost. https://www.huffpost.com/entry/your-destiny-is-determined-by-your-decisions_b_610874ffe4b0497e67026e56

Kramer, A. D. I., Guillory, J. E., & Hancock, J. T. (2014). Experimental evidence of massive-scale emotional contagion through social networks. Proceedings of the National Academy of Sciences, 111(24), 8788–8790. https://www.pnas.org/content/111/24/8788#ref-3

Krauss Whitbourne, S. (2012). The Definitive Guide to Guilt. Psychology Today. https://www.psychologytoday.com/us/blog/fulfillment-any-age/201208/the-definitive-guide-guilt

Lamberts, C. (2016, October 31). The words you attach to your experience become your experience. She's the Curly Girl. https://shesthecurlygirl.wordpress.com/2016/10/31/the-words-you-attach-to-your-experience-become-your-experience/

Lamothe, C. (2019, November 22). How to Stop Being Insecure and Build Self-Esteem. Healthline. https://www.healthline.com/health/how-to-stop-being-insecure

Langley, E. (2018, July 10). How to get over heartbreak: the ultimate guide. BBC Three. https://www.bbc.co.uk/bbcthree/article/996edc30-d6e9-480b-b4a8-15b626f0aa76

Langley, T., & Scarlet, J. (2015, June 24). Inside Out: Emotional Truths by Way of Pixar. Psychology Today. https://www.psychologytoday.com/us/blog/beyond-heroes-and-villains/201506/inside-out-emotional-truths-way-pixar

Langsleg, S. J. E., & Sanchez, M. E. (2018). APA PsycNet. Psycnet.apa.org. https://psycnet.apa.org/doiLanding?doi=10.1037%2Fxge0000360

LaPier, R. R. (2018, November 3). How the Loss of Native American Languages Affects Our Understanding of the Natural World. Truthout. https://truthout.org/articles/how-the-loss-of-native-american-languages-affects-our-understanding-of-nature/

Li, C. (2020, September 5). The Life Lessons That "High School Drama" Had Taught Me. Medium. https://medium.com/the-ascent/the-life-lessons-that-high-school-drama-had-taught-me-396cae46f6fc

Lifecoachonthego. (2012, July 26). 10 Top Questions to Identify Your Strengths - Without The Struggle! Life Coach on the Go. https://lifecoachonthego.com/10-questions-to-identify-your-strengths-without-struggle/

Lindberg, S. (2018, July 24). 12 Tips for Forgiving Yourself. Healthline. https://www.healthline.com/health/how-to-forgive-yourself#1.-Focus-on-your-emotions

Lokos, A. (2010). A quote from Pocket Peace. Www.goodreads.com. https://www.goodreads.com/quotes/

424358-don-t-believe-everything-you-think-thoughts-are-just-that--

Lotzof, K. (2018). Are we really made of stardust? Nhm.ac.uk. https://www.nhm.ac.uk/discover/are-we-really-made-of-stardust.html

Louisiana Civil Service. (n.d.). SWOT Analysis: Questions for Conducting a Personal Analysis. https://www.civilservice.louisiana.gov/files/divisions/Training/Job%20Aid/Supervisor%20Toolbox/Questions%20for%20Personal%20SWOT.pdf

Lui, E., & Wikihow. (n.d.). How to Know if You Are Ready for a Relationship. WikiHow. Retrieved August 4, 2021, from https://www.wikihow.com/Know-if-You-Are-Ready-for-a-Relationship

Macy, A. (2018, October 30). 3 Signs You Have an "Upper Limit" Problem. Www.workingagainstgravity.com. https://www.workingagainstgravity.com/articles/3-signs-you-have-an-upper-limit-problem

Manson, M. (2015, December 25). Toxic relationship habits most people think are normal. Quartz. https://qz.com/580940/toxic-relationship-habits-most-people-think-are-normal/

MAriyah. (n.d.). Gimme Shelter (2013) - IMDb. Www.imdb.com. Retrieved July 24, 2021, from https://www.imdb.com/title/tt1657510/

Martin Lillie, C. M. (2016, December 30). Be kind to yourself: How self-compassion can improve your resiliency. Mayo Clinic. https://www.mayoclinic.org/healthy-lifestyle/

adult-health/in-depth/self-compassion-can-improve-your-resiliency/art-20267193

Mayo Clinic Staff. (2017). Forgiveness. Mayo Clinic; https://www.mayoclinic.org/healthy-lifestyle/adult-health/in-depth/forgiveness/art-20047692

Merriam-Webster. (2021). Definition of Mantra. Www.merriam-Webster.com. https://www.merriam-webster.com/dictionary/mantra#other-words

Mind UK. (2021, February). What causes anxiety problems. Www.mind.org.uk. https://www.mind.org.uk/information-support/types-of-mental-health-problems/anxiety-and-panic-attacks/causes/

Moore, C. (2019, March 4). Positive Daily Affirmations: Is There Science Behind It? PositivePsychology.com. https://positivepsychology.com/daily-affirmations/

Morty Lefkoe. (2010). The Lefkoe Institute – How Our Language Determines Our Reality. Mortylefkoe.com. https://www.mortylefkoe.com/how-our-language-determines-our-reality/

Mutziger, A. L., John. (2021, March 21). 5 steps to get over a breakup, according to therapists. Insider. https://www.insider.com/how-to-get-over-a-breakup

Naab, K. (2014, February 2). The True Story Behind "Gimme Shelter." Aleteia — Catholic Spirituality, Lifestyle, World News, and Culture. https://aleteia.org/2014/02/02/the-true-story-behind-gimme-shelter/2/

Naikan Retreat Centre. (n.d.). Release the pain of the past and fear of the future. Naikan Retreat Centre. Retrieved August 6, 2021, from https://naikan.co.uk/

National Centre for Complimentary and Integrative Health. (2016, April). Meditation: In Depth. NCCIH. https://www.nccih.nih.gov/health/meditation-in-depth

Neff, A. J. (2019, July 15). Do Mantras Work? Medium. https://medium.com/interfaith-now/do-mantras-work-60000859f5b5

New Zealand Government Health and Safety Authority. (2018). Mental Health Pocketbook. https://www.healthandsafety.govt.nz/assets/Documents/Mental_Health_Pocketbook.pdf

NHS. (2021, February 10). How it works - Cognitive behavioural therapy (CBT). Nhs.uk. https://www.nhs.uk/mental-health/talking-therapies-medicine-treatments/talking-therapies-and-counselling/cognitive-behavioural-therapy-cbt/how-it-works/

Online Etymology Dictionary. (n.d.). environ | Origin and meaning of environ by Online Etymology Dictionary. Www.etymonline.com. Retrieved August 5, 2021, from https://www.etymonline.com/word/environ?ref=etymonline_crossreference#etymonline_v_38237

Paylor, J. (2011). Volunteering and health: evidence of impact and implications for policy and review. Institution for Volunteering Research.

Pellerin, N., Raufaste, E., & Dambrun, M. (2020). Selflessness and Happiness in Everyday Life. Journal of Individual Differences, 42(3), 1–9. https://doi.org/10.1027/1614-

0001/a000335

PESTLEanalysis Contributor. (2016, June 21). Why SWOT Analysis is Essential in Personal Development. PESTLE Analysis. https://pestleanalysis.com/swot-analysis-in-personal-development/

Petrone, P. (2017, December 5). How to Determine Your Strengths? 21 Questions to Ask Yourself. Www.linkedin.com. https://www.linkedin.com/business/learning/blog/career-success-tips/21-questions-that-will-help-you-determine-your-strengths-goals

Phillips, C. (2017, April 20). 11 Ways to Take Charge of Your Life. HuffPost. https://www.huffpost.com/entry/11-ways-to-take-charge-of-your-life_b_58f899c7e4b0b6ca13416160

Pickhardt, C. E. (2012). Adolescence and the Development of Habits. Psychology Today. https://www.psychologytoday.com/us/blog/surviving-your-childs-adolescence/201201/adolescence-and-the-development-habits

Positive Affirmation Center. (2021). 10 Powerful Positive Affirmations for Teens. Positiveaffirmationscenter.com. https://positiveaffirmationscenter.com/positive-affirmations-for-teens/

PsychologyToday. (2019). Forgiveness | Psychology Today. Psychology Today. https://www.psychologytoday.com/us/basics/forgiveness

Puddicombe, A. (2012, November 27). What Is a Beautiful Mind? | Psychology Today. Www.psychologytoday.com. https://www.psychologytoday.com/us/blog/get-some-headspace/201211/what-is-beautiful-mind

Quote Investigator. (2016, April 26). If You Always Do What You've Always Done, You Always Get What You've Always Gotten – Quote Investigator. Quoteinvestigator.com. https://quoteinvestigator.com/2016/04/25/get/

Quote Investigator. (2017, October 24). Be the Change You Wish To See in the World – Quote Investigator. Quoteinvestigator.com. https://quoteinvestigator.com/2017/10/23/be-change/

Reachout Australia. (n.d.). A step-by-step guide to problem solving. Au.reachout.com. https://au.reachout.com/articles/a-step-by-step-guide-to-problem-solving

Reis, R. (2019). The Socratic Method: What it is and How to Use it in the Classroom | Tomorrow's Professor Postings. Stanford.edu. https://tomprof.stanford.edu/posting/810

Reynolds, G. (2018, May 2). News: Even a Little Exercise Might Make Us... (The New York Times) - Behind the headlines - NLM. NCBI. https://www.ncbi.nlm.nih.gov/search/research-news/2097/

Rose, S. (2020, April 1). Do Positive Affirmations Work? A Look at the Science. Steve Rose, PhD. https://steverosephd.com/do-positive-affirmations-work/

Salovey, P., Rothman, A. J., Detweiler, J. B., & Steward, W. T. (2000). Emotional states and physical health. American Psychologist, 55(1), 110–121. https://doi.org/10.1037/0003-066x.55.1.110

Sarkhedi, B. (2017, January 6). 10 Simple Ways To Get Over Your Heartbreak. Lifehack. https://www.lifehack.org/518275/10-simple-ways-get-over-your-heartbreak

Sharma, A., Madaan, V., & Petty, F. D. (2006). Exercise for mental health. Primary Care Companion to the Journal of Clinical Psychiatry, 8(2), 106. https://www.ncbi.nlm.nih.gov/pmc/articles/PMC1470658/

Shuda, D. (2020, September 23). How To Become More Courageous in Your Daily Life. Everyday Power. https://everydaypower.com/how-to-become-more-courageous/

Shuman, C. (2021, July 16). How to Break the Cycle of Negative Thinking | Psychology Today. Www.psychologytoday.com. https://www.psychologytoday.com/us/blog/trial-triumph/202107/how-break-the-cycle-negative-thinking

Sider, M., & Dubin-McKnight, K. (2021, June 3). How CBT Can Help Us Make Sense of Suffering | Psychology Today. Www.psychologytoday.com. https://www.psychologytoday.com/us/blog/pain-loss-and-suffering/202106/how-cbt-can-help-us-make-sense-suffering

Sidor, M., & Dubin, K. (2020, November 9). Can We Cease Suffering? | Psychology Today. Www.psychologytoday.com. https://www.psychologytoday.com/us/blog/pain-loss-and-suffering/202011/can-we-cease-suffering

Simeona, M. (n.d.-a). Dr. Ihaleakala Hew Len - Discover His Famous Ho'oponopono Story. The Hawaiian Healing Prayer Ho'oponopono. Retrieved August 6, 2021, from https://hooponoponomiracle.com/dr-ihaleakala-hew-len/

Simeona, M. (n.d.-b). Ho'oponopono Technique - How To Practice The Hawaiian Self Healing Process. The Hawaiian Healing Prayer Ho'oponopono. Retrieved August 5, 2021, from https://hooponoponomiracle.com/ho-oponopono-technique/

Smith, J. A. (2013). Six Habits of Highly Grateful People. Greater Good. https://greatergood.berkeley.edu/article/item/six_habits_of_highly_grateful_people

Sosienski, S. (2011, March 29). How to Stop Gossiping and Creating Drama. Tiny Buddha. https://tinybuddha.com/blog/how-to-stop-gossiping-and-creating-drama/

Staples, J. (2019, May 17). Done Right Podcast Episode 3. Donerightpodcast.org. https://www.workfront.com/campaigns/done-right-podcast/episode-3

Steiner, C. J., & Reisinger, Y. (2006). Understanding existential authenticity. Annals of Tourism Research, 33(2), 299–318. https://doi.org/10.1016/j.annals.2005.08.002

Styzek, K., & Wikihow. (2021, June 10). How to Deal With Drama. WikiHow. https://www.wikihow.com/Deal-With-Drama

Team Tony. (2016, December 27). Learn How to Ask Questions and Better Yourself Every Day. Tonyrobbins.com. https://www.tonyrobbins.com/mind-meaning/ask-better-questions/

Telles, S., Kumar, S., Nagendra, H., Manjunath, N., & Naveen, K. (2010). Meditation on OM: Relevance from ancient texts and contemporary science. International Journal of Yoga, 3(1), 2. https://doi.org/10.4103/0973-6131.66771

The Freedom Writers Foundation. (n.d.). About the Freedom Writers Foundation. Http://Www.freedomwritersfoundation.org/. Retrieved August 10, 2021, from http://www.freedomwritersfoundation.org/about/#freedomwriters

Thorn, A. (2018, August 3). Why Do I Hate My Self? | Philosophy Tube ★. Www.youtube.com. https://www.youtube.com/watch?v=0AuFvboGKrQ

Tolle, E. (2010). Eckhart Tolle Quote. A-Z Quotes. https://www.azquotes.com/quote/809276

Tracy, N. (2012, May 3). Guilt and Mental Illness: Feeling Guilty Is Overrated, HealthyPlace. Retrieved on 2021, August 4 from https://www.healthyplace.com/blogs/breakingbipolar/2012/05/guilt-and-mental-illness

UN Environmental Programme. (2017, July 21). Indigenous people and nature: a tradition of conservation. UN Environment. https://www.unep.org/news-and-stories/story/indigenous-people-and-nature-tradition-conservation

US Department of Health and Human Services. (2018). Physical Activity Guidelines for Americans 2 nd edition. https://health.gov/sites/default/files/2019-09/Physical_Activity_Guidelines_2nd_edition.pdf#page=39

Van Dam, N. T., van Vugt, M. K., Vago, D. R., Schmalzl, L., Saron, C. D., Olendzki, A., Meissner, T., Lazar, S. W., Kerr, C. E., Gorchov, J., Fox, K. C. R., Field, B. A., Britton, W. B., Brefczynski-Lewis, J. A., & Meyer, D. E. (2018). Mind the Hype: A Critical Evaluation and Prescriptive Agenda for Research on Mindfulness and Meditation. Perspectives on Psychological Science : A Journal of the Association for Psychological Science, 13(1), 36–61. https://doi.org/10.1177/1745691617709589

Warner, I. (2020, December 18). 50 Inspirational Sailing Quotes. Habit Stacker. https://thehabitstacker.com/sailing-quotes/

Watson, A. M. (2017). Sleep and Athletic Performance. Current Sports Medicine Reports, 16(6), 413–418. https://doi.org/10.1249/jsr.0000000000000418

Watson, S. (2011, June 21). Are You Ready to Go Out? WebMD; WebMD. https://teens.webmd.com/features/teen-dating-relationship-questions

Watson, S. (2015, October 30). Volunteering may be good for body and mind - Harvard Health Blog. Harvard Health Blog. https://www.health.harvard.edu/blog/volunteering-may-be-good-for-body-and-mind-201306266428

Weisner, L. (2021, June 4). Confidence Coaching for Adolescent Girls | Psychology Today. Www.psychologytoday.com. https://www.psychologytoday.com/us/blog/the-venn-diagram-life/202106/confidence-coaching-adolescent-girls

Whitener, S. (2018, May 9). Council Post: How Your Emotions Influence Your Decisions. Forbes. https://www.forbes.com/sites/forbescoachescouncil/2018/05/09/how-your-emotions-influence-your-decisions/

Wikihow, & Griffin, T. (n.d.). How to Get Over Heartbreak. WikiHow. Retrieved August 1, 2021, from https://www.wikihow.com/Get-Over-Heartbreak

wikiHow, & Kouzmenko, M. (2005, February 24). Meditate. WikiHow; wikiHow. https://www.wikihow.com/Meditate

WikiHow. (n.d.). How to Use Autosuggestion. WikiHow. Retrieved August 7, 2021, from https://www.wikihow.com/Use-Autosuggestion

wikiHow, & Tura, N. (2008, March 16). Give Advice. WikiHow; wikiHow. https://www.wikihow.com/Give-Advice

WomensMedia, & Miller, J. (2016, July 8). 8 Ways To Have More Gratitude Every Day. Forbes. https://www.forbes.com/sites/womensmedia/2016/07/08/8-ways-to-have-more-gratitude-every-day/?sh=192033b81d54

Worthington, E. (n.d.). REACH Forgiveness. Everett Worthington. Retrieved August 4, 2021, from http://www.evworthington-forgiveness.com/reach-forgiveness/

Yeager, D. S., Romero, C., Paunesku, D., Hulleman, C. S., Schneider, B., Hinojosa, C., Lee, H. Y., O'Brien, J., Flint, K., Roberts, A., Trott, J., Greene, D., Walton, G. M., & Dweck, C. S. (2016). Using design thinking to improve psychological interventions: The case of the growth mindset during the transition to high school. Journal of Educational Psychology, 108(3), 374–391. https://doi.org/10.1037/edu0000098

Yee, A. (2015, November 29). The Upper Limit Problem: What's Holding You Back In Your Life? HuffPost. https://www.huffpost.com/entry/the-upper-limit-problem-w_b_8654262

Yellowberry. (n.d.). Our Mantras. Yellowberry. Retrieved July 24, 2021, from https://www.yellowberrycompany.com/pages/our-mantras

Yetman, D. (2020, August 28). Why Does Stretching Feel Good? Benefits and Why It Feels Good (L. Jarmursz, Ed.). Healthline. https://www.healthline.com/health/why-does-stretching-feel-good#why-it-feels-good

youth.gov. (2000). Characteristics of Healthy & Unhealthy Relationships | Youth.gov. Youth.gov. https://youth.gov/youth-topics/teen-dating-violence/characteristics

www.ingramcontent.com/pod-product-compliance
Lightning Source LLC
Chambersburg PA
CBHW072008290426
44109CB00018B/2173